THE EPICS OF E▮▮▮

A graphic and chil▮▮▮▮▮▮▮▮▮▮▮▮▮▮▮▮▮▮▮▮▮ to reach
the top of Mt. Everest climax in a detailed study of the Hillary-
Tensing triumph of 1953. An absorbing narrative of courage
and tenacity, the story of Everest will grip every reader.

LEONARD WIBBERLEY

born in Dublin and educated early in the Gaelic language, did
not learn English until he was in his teens. Then he read
TREASURE ISLAND, his favorite book, and the one to which he
attributes his early inspiration to be a writer. His works include THE MOUSE THAT ROARED, published in 1959 and made
into a motion picture. Now a resident of California, Mr. Wibberley has most recently published historical novels rooted in
American history.

LAUREL-LEAF MAYFLOWER BOOKS

are a new series designed especially to entertain and enlighten
young people. The finest contemporary mystery, adventure, ro-
mance and action novels, as well as exciting non-fiction, form
a singular list of books for leisure reading. The series is prepared under the direction of M. Jerry Weiss, Chairman, English
Department, Jersey City State College; Charles Reasoner, Asso-
ciate Professor, Elementary Education, New York University;
and Ned E. Hoopes, Instructor, Hunter College High School and
Hunter College.

Other titles available in Laurel-Leaf Mayflower Books

LEONARD WIBBERLEY

THE EPICS OF EVEREST

LAUREL-LEAF LIBRARY

A MAYFLOWER BOOK

Published by DELL PUBLISHING CO., INC.
750 Third Avenue, New York, N. Y. 10017
Copyright 1954 by Leonard Wibberley
Laurel ® TM 674623, Dell Publishing Co., Inc.
All rights reserved.
Reprinted by arrangement with Farrar, Straus & Giroux, Inc.
First Dell printing—April, 1966
Printed in U. S. A.

Acknowledgment

THE AUTHOR WISHES TO EXPRESS HIS GRAT-
itude to the following leaders of Everest expeditions
who kindly gave him permission to draw upon their
published works in compiling this book.

Hugh Ruttledge, for permission to use material
from his book *Attack on Everest* (McBride, New
York); Harold W. Tilman, *Mount Everest, 1938*
(Cambridge University Press); Eric Shipton and the
Himalaya Committee of the Royal Geographical
Society, London, *The Mount Everest Reconnaissance
Expedition, 1951* (Hodder and Stoughton, London).

In addition, the author wishes to thank the editors
of *Life* magazine for their permission to obtain the
facts of the final successful climb of Mount Everest
which were given in the issue of *Life* of June 29, 1953.
Edward Arnold & Co., publishers, of London also gave
permission to use material from the following works
published by them: *Mount Everest: the Reconnaissance, 1921* by Lt. Col. C. K. Howard-Bury, D.S.O.
and other members of the expedition; *The Assault on
Mount Everest, 1922* by the Hon. C. G. Bruce and
other members of the expedition; *The Fight for
Everest, 1924* by Lt. Col. E. F. Norton, D.S.O. and
other members of the expedition.

A complete bibliography of all works drawn upon in compiling this book is given at the end of the volume.

Leonard Wibberley

Hermosa Beach
California

CONTENTS

CHAPTER ONE

The Finding of the Mountain

TOWERING ABOVE THE WORLD'S HIGHEST range of mountains, the Himalayas, there is one lonely, supreme peak, biting higher into the heavens than any other upon earth. It is surrounded, like a great fortress or citadel of Nature, by the most formidable barriers, some visible, others invisible. The mountain is called Everest, or in the language of the Tibetans in whose country it partly lies, Chomo Lungma, the "Goddess Mother of the World." Around it are huge glaciers and cliffs of ice, precipices that plunge thousands of feet, chasms and treacherous slopes of snow which, though they seem firm, may avalanche at any time.

The glaciers, the ice fields, the precipices and chasms are the visible defenses of this mountain against attack by Man. The invisible defenses are even more perilous. They consist of winds which reach a force of one hundred and more miles an hour; air so thin that men lose their senses if they penetrate it without adequate preparations, and light so fierce that eyes and skin must be protected from it.

That this mountain was the world's highest was unknown until 1849 when Sir George Everest, Surveyor General of India, was engaged in making a survey of the peaks of the Himalaya range.

His survey of the mountains was conducted with scientific instruments placed miles away in India, for much of the Himalayas lie in what was then, and still is today, the Forbidden Land of Tibet. Why Tibet is called the Forbidden Land is explained later. Sir George and his assistants did not make any special note of Everest at the time they took their sights of the peak from the stations which they set up. They merely recorded the mountain as Peak XV and entered under that heading the scientific observations which they had made regarding it. It was not until three years later, when Sir George had retired from the post of Surveyor General, that these observations were worked out and translated into feet above sea level.

Then one day in 1852, a member of the India Trigonometrical Survey burst into the office of Sir Andrew Waugh, who had succeeded Sir George as Surveyor General and cried, "Sir. Sir. We have found the greatest mountain in the world. Peak XV. It is 29,002 feet high!"

The findings were checked by sights taken from six different points and the observations worked out with the greatest care. But there could be no doubt about it. Peak XV was the world's highest point—a soaring 29,002 feet above sea level. It was named Mount Everest after Sir George Everest and its position filled in on the world's maps.

It may seem surprising that so long a time elapsed before Mount Everest was recognized as the world's highest peak.

But Everest is part of a system of giant mountains. And being more distant from India than many of its companion peaks, the mountain seems, when viewed from afar, to be smaller than they are. Indeed, as you travel towards it, Everest disappears, blocked out behind smaller giants which are nearer. Only when these have been negotiated does the majestic mountain appear, towering above the clouds into the blue vault of the sky, its rocky peak, capped with ice and snow, alternately flashing in the sun and then blocked out by clouds which form suddenly around it and as suddenly disappear.

Mount Everest does not lie wholly in Tibet. The southern face of the mountain is in the adjoining Kingdom of Nepal. Both countries hold the mountain in the highest reverence. And both countries traditionally exclude strangers from their territory. Nepal and Tibet were therefore largely unmapped when Everest was found to be the world's highest mountain. And the prospects of mapping them, and of finding the best way to approach Mount Everest, were remote indeed. If anything further about the mountain was to be discovered, spies would have to slip into either Nepal or Tibet or both, living from hand to mouth and in constant danger of imprisonment or even death. In Tibet the dangers confronting anyone trying to enter the land secretly were particularly numerous. The people, deeply religious, are led by Lamas, who are priests of the Buddhist religion, which is the faith of Tibet. The Tibetan Buddhists are under the control of the Dalai Lama, who lives in a monastery at Lhasa, the capital. Almost every aspect of the lives of the Tibetans is governed by their religion. They believe that they must be born again and again, sometimes to a better life and sometimes to a more miserable one, until at last they achieve perfection on earth and are admitted to Nirvana, or heaven.

For centuries the Lamas taught the people that the land in which they lived was an earthly paradise, desired by all nations. They told them that foreigners would seek to enter and take possession of their land, and they must never allow any in. To do so would be a great sin which would, on their death, bring them a rebirth in a very miserable condition. All the passes into Tibet were therefore guarded by fortresses and military outposts. Monasteries, perched high on mountain peaks, overlooked the bleak valleys so that all who came and went could be seen. Foreigners who entered and were caught were imprisoned, and frequently made into slaves. For these reasons, Tibet became known as the Forbidden Land.

But the India Survey Office, now that it had discovered the highest mountain in the world, was determined to find out more about it. In 1861, a certain Captain Montgomery of the India Survey Office was training Indians in surveying methods in order that they might penetrate into Tibet as spies to find out more about Mount Everest.

Obviously his spies could not take openly with them any surveying instruments. They were to enter the country disguised as pilgrims, for despite the ban on strangers, many Buddhists from neighboring lands were and still are allowed to make pilgrimages to sacred shrines in Tibet. But Captain Montgomery devised a number of ways in which his scouts could do their surveying while appearing to be doing something very different. The Tibetans, when praying, use an instrument called a prayer wheel. This, in its smaller size, is a cylinder on the end of a stick. Prayers written on a roll of paper are placed on the cylinder. Each time the cylinder or wheel is turned around prayers are believed to go to heaven. Captain Montgomery put inside the cylinder a blank roll of paper on which observations could be made. Then he instructed his men to make one revolution of the wheel for every step they took. They would appear to be praying, but in actuality, they would be measuring, quite accurately, the distance which they had traveled.

Another method of measuring distance made use of strings of beads. These are also used by the Tibetans to count their prayers. Captain Montgomery trained his men to use them to count their footsteps—one bead to a hundred paces. To some he gave staffs, such as pilgrims carry, to help them over the rocks of the passes and the mountains. Inside the staffs were boiling point thermometers with which they could measure atmospheric pressure and so discover how high they were above sea level at different places.

Such then were the pioneers of Mount Everest for the western world. They were men who could scarcely speak English and had no scientific training beyond that which they needed for their jobs. Yet they undertook perilous journeys quite alone, for very little pay and with no prospect of fame, to further the world's knowledge of its greatest mountain.

Perhaps it is not quite true to say that they went into Tibet solely to seek out the approaches to Everest. Certainly that was one of the most important tasks assigned to many of them. But the India Survey was also interested in filling in blanks in the map represented by both Nepal and Tibet. They wanted to trace the course of rivers which rose in the Himalayas and flowed into India, to discover the locations of valleys and passes and many other things. All these were part of the job. But Everest was the lodestone which drew the men on.

So secret was their work and so dangerous that the names of these Indians and other Asiatic explorers were not given out until much later. They were kept from all except those in the India Survey who had to know them. Instead of names the men were given initals by which they were known.

Thus one, Nain Singh, was known to the India Survey only as A.K. He, on his first journey, made his way to the Tibetan capital of Lhasa. Hari Ram, who was assigned the job of journeying in the direction of

Mount Everest, was given the initials M.H. Frequently these explorers were set upon by robbers, or
deserted in the Tibetan plateau by caravans to which
they had attached themselves. Sometimes they were
left in the wilderness without a morsel of food to eat.
Yet they never wavered. Nain Singh, for instance, was
in Tibet for four years without a word being heard of
him. He was given up for dead. Then he reappeared
in India after having made his way across Tibet into
China and then back by way of Indo China. His
survey contributed greatly to knowledge of the geog-
raphy of Tibet.

Hari Ram entered Tibet disguised as a pilgrim,
carrying around his neck a small amulet which was in
reality a compass. He reached Dingri, north of
Everest, after crossing a twenty-thousand-foot pass.
But he found his way blocked by impassable peaks
and so was forced to return.

Perhaps the most remarkable story of these early
"pundit pioneers," as they came to be called, was that
of an Indian explorer, Kintup, whose task, assigned to
him by the India Survey, was to trace the course of
the Tibetan river Tsampo (or Tsangpo).

It was theorized that this was the same river which
in India is called the Brahmaputra. Kintup's job was
to follow the Tsampo in Tibet. He was to throw blocks
of wood, cut in a special way, into the river. A watch
would be kept in India, day and night, on the Brahmaputra for these blocks which would tell if they
arrived that the two rivers were the same. But after
Kintup had reached Tibet, not a single block of wood
was seen, though a close watch of the river was kept
for several months.

Then Captain Harmon, the officer who had sent
Kintup on his mission, fell ill and went home to En-

gland. After that the guard on the river was relaxed and eventually dropped. None of Kintup's blocks was ever seen and all hope for him was abandoned. It was thought that shortly after crossing into Tibet, he must have been taken prisoner and killed or had met death by accident.

What had actually happened, however, was that Kintup had been taken prisoner and had worked as a slave for the Tibetans for four long years. Then he escaped after suffering terrible hardships. A man of less resolution would have made his way quickly back to the safety of India. But Kintup was determined that he would complete the task he had set out to achieve. So he doggedly followed the Tsampo river, made himself a supply of the wooden blocks as had been agreed, and commenced to throw them into the stream. The blocks floated down into India but nobody was watching for them, the guard on the river having been given up two years previously. The indomitable Kintup continued along the stream, constantly in danger of being recaptured and once more being made a slave.

When he finally returned to India no one would believe the story of his wanderings because it was so fantastic. But eventually all he had to say was shown to be true, and much light was thrown on the course of the Brahmaputra through the Forbidden Land of Tibet. It was shown that the Brahmaputra and the Tsampo were one and the same river.

Tibet now became a magnet for adventurers from many lands. A dozen or more people in the final decade of the last century penetrated the country, most of them seeking to get to Lhasa, the capital which became known as the Forbidden City, for no white man had ever been allowed to enter it. W. W.

Rockhill, an American, was among those who journeyed secretly into the country to gain further knowledge of it and its people. But in the meantime events were shaping up which foreshadowed the day when the barriers around Tibet would have to be partially lowered. The country, at the time under the domination of China, was being eyed by Russia. It had been for many years part of British policy to prevent the Russians from taking control of Tibet, which would bring them to the back door of India.

In 1903 Russian penetration into Tibet was sufficiently disturbing for the British to attempt to establish close relations with the central Tibetan government in Lhasa. The Dalai Lama, ruler of the land, repudiated all requests that he receive a British mission to discuss the situation. Accordingly Lieutenant Colonel Francis Younghusband was ordered to undertake a mission to Lhasa and was provided with an armed escort who would see that he got through. The escort was reinforced after some weeks, a few skirmishes were fought with the Tibetan soldiery, and Col. Younghusband eventually reached Lhasa. There he concluded a treaty with the Dalai Lama which opened two Tibetan cities as foreign trade markets and abolished payments of trade dues between India and Tibet.

That was the opening wedge in gaining entry to Tibet. Later the Chinese invaded Tibet to restore their control over the land, and the Dalai Lama fled to Darjeeling in British India. There he was well received and treated. On his return to Tibet, a measure of mutual friendship and trust had developed between Tibet and Britain. This proved to be the key which would unlock the doors to Everest. But much was to happen before an assault against the world's highest peak could be mounted.

CHAPTER TWO

Lone Venture

JUST BEFORE THE OUTBREAK OF WORLD
War I, two men, quite unknown to each other, were
laying the first practical steps for the assaults on
Mount Everest which were to follow years later.

The first of these was a young officer in the British
Army, serving in India. His name was Captain John
B. Noel. He had spent a great many of his leaves from
the Army not back home in England as most of his
fellow officers did, but exploring the Himalaya mountains and the valleys which threaded between them.
For years he dreamed of striking out into Tibet to find
the path to Mount Everest. But the difficulties which
lay in the way were formidable. As a white man, he
would be readily recognized. As an army officer he
could get into serious trouble by crossing into a land
whose frontiers were closed to foreigners and whose
friendship the British government was very anxious to
retain.

Captain Noel thought long and hard about the prospects of getting secretly into Tibet and to the foot of
Mount Everest. At last he could resist the urge no
longer. He obtained a leave of absence from the Army,
and recruited three hillmen from the Tibetan borders
with whom he had done some exploring in the past.
His plan was to set out from Darjeeling in India and,
disguised as a Mohammedan from India, enter Tibet,

avoiding villages and towns, and strike out in the direction of Everest. A Mohammedan from India would arouse suspicion in Tibet and be turned out when caught. But he would not be so quickly discovered as a white man.

Accordingly in the spring of 1913, Captain Noel made his way to Darjeeling, where he picked up his three native companions and made the final preparations for his adventure. He decided that he must be free to wander about the countryside and so could not travel with much luggage. Yet he had to be prepared to meet bitter cold and piercing winds, and at the same time protect himself and his party against the Tibetans. He took with him two tin trunks, such as could be bought cheaply in a native bazaar. In these he packed two cameras, mapping instruments, a boiling point thermometer with which to measure altitude, an American rifle which could be taken to pieces, plenty of ammunition and blankets. He carried on his person his army revolver (well hidden) and had automatic pistols for his men. These together with two native tents completed his stores.

For the first part of the journey he bought some ponies which would have to be left behind later, for they would not be able to find food in the frozen Tibetan plateau.

Darjeeling is one of the hill stations of India, a resort city situated on a peak overlooking a valley choked with the teeming growth of the tropics. He would have to descend into this valley and climb out the other side to get to the border of Tibet. The journey down the valley and out again was an adventure in itself. At times, Noel and his companions were set upon by fat tropical leeches, which live in the rank jungle growth or on the branches of trees overhead. The leeches are quite blind, and yet have some instinct which tells them unerringly that warm-blooded creatures are passing by. As the men passed below, in the forest gloom, the leeches would swing their soft bodies out to drop unerring upon them. Picking them off was useless. Those removed were replaced by others. Noel and his men just had to become used to the horror of them.

Then there were hordes of insects which stung all exposed surfaces of the skin, setting up an unbearable itch.

At one place Noel's way led over a gorge which could be crossed only by a suspension bridge of ropes and steel wire. The bridge was so flimsy that it swung wildly with every step, threatening to drop the men hundreds of feet into the gully below. But there were compensations as they climbed out of the valley. Thick vines and tangled undergrowth gave way to pleasant woods of rhododendron, larch, and pine. Higher up still, mountain flowers, cool air, and cold crystal streams made the men wonder whether it was only a few days ago that they had been plucking off the jungle leeches in the oppressive humid air of the valley.

Up they went then to a tableland thirteen thousand feet above sea level and only a few miles from the Tibetan border. Here the men Captain Noel had brought with him became fearful of the hazards which lay ahead. They were for going back, saying there wasn't one among them who knew his way through the mountains ahead. But Noel assured them he had a map which would be easy to follow. He had a map indeed, but he himself could not put much faith in it for it was little more than a sketch, He managed to allay the fears of the men, however, and even recruited four or five others as reinforcement.

By climbing to the top of a nearby peak, Noel was

able to get a view of the great waste of mountains ahead, all snow-covered, in the heart of which lay Everest. The first problem was to find a pass into Tibet which would not be guarded. The obvious pass was one on which lay a Tibetan fortress called Kampa Dzong. No one could go up this pass without being seen and challenged by the soldiers. To the west, between him and Tibet, lay Mount Kinchinjunga, a peak only one thousand feet short of Everest. Noel decided to pass behind this in the hope that on the further side there might be a way into the Forbidden Land.

He set out with his party, carrying fourteen days' food supply, his face stained to make him look like a native of India. The first day they struggled up a rough stony valley to sixteen thousand feet and spent the night in a cave. Far below were the pasture lands where the Tibetan shepherds brought their flocks to graze in the summer. Around towered mountains of stone and snow and ice—silent and menacing—their colors constantly changing through all shades of blue, green, and violet with the setting sun.

Here, Captain Noel got his first taste of the Tibetan climate. The sun's rays during the day, pouring down from directly overhead, parched his lips and were so hot that they raised blisters on his skin. But as soon as the sun went behind a fleeting cloud, all was deathly cold. It was much like being plunged from a furnace into an ice bath, and all within the space of seconds. And when, with the sun clouded over, the wind blew, it could be felt through the thickest clothing, merciless and cold.

The next stage of their journey took Captain Noel and his companions across the Chorten Nyim Pass—a pass so steep and so strewn with boulders of gigantic size that it was no longer used by the Tibetan tribesmen. For this reason Captain Noel selected this pass to cross into Tibet, since it would not be guarded. But the going was wearying in the extreme. The way in many places was blocked by snow and by massive stones which had fallen down from the peaks overhead in rock avalanches. There was always the uncomfortable thought that more rocks might come plunging down from thousands of feet above at any moment. The air became so thin that one of the men bled from the nose and all complained of headaches.

The air in the pass was what mountaineers describe as "dead." It had lain so long cooped up, boxed in by the cliffs of ice which rose hundreds of feet overhead that it was stagnant and seemed incapable of supporting life. The natives call this air Zhidag, or the evil breath of the spirit of mountains, for they believe all mountains inhabited by spirits both good and bad. At last, after scrambling over steep slopes of stone and finding a way around or over the pinacles of ice studding the pass, they got to the top.

Once the top had been reached, the party faced the problem of descending to the plateau below. Much of Tibet consists of a tableland with an average height of fourteen thousand feet. Noel and his men were several thousand feet above this tableland and had to descend into the desolate flatlands, down rocky ledges, over great cracks, some of them filled with soft treacherous snow, and down slopes of solid ice on which it was almost impossible to gain a foothold. Several hours still were needed to get to a glacier below and there the party camped, listening to the wind howling past the ice pinacles around them, and huddled together for warmth. Their breath froze on the edges of their blankets and only exhaustion permitted them to get any sleep at all.

The next morning they decided to go on to the

shrine of Chorten Nyim which is cared for by Tibetan nuns. There they could hope to get directions and perhaps some extra food. When they entered the shrine, Captain Noel picked out a dark corner and sat down in it, for it was essential that he avoid being recognized as a foreigner. As it turned out, the leader of the nuns and two of her assistants were blind, so the danger was not great.

The nuns bade them all make sacrifices to the shrine, which they did, placing grains of rice in some bowls under the images of the Tibetan gods. The nuns gave them yak milk and some food, and said they would pray for them, for they were ignorant and worldly men. Then Noel and his companions left with no new directions but at least with a good meal inside them.

Noel decided to try to find the way from the barren Tibetan desert, so flat that travelers on it could be seen from a great distance, into the valleys of Nepal where it would be easier to avoid being discovered. The only exit of which he had heard was a pass called Langpoo, but he was quite uncertain in what direction it lay. He believed that the pass was somewhere to the west, and so the group marched westward for some time, staying to the hilly parts as much as they could, though this made travel infinitely more difficult. They walked miles out of their route trying to find a a way over one particular canyon, and eventually decided to descend into it in the hope that they could walk out by following its length. But this proved impossible and they were compelled to climb back out again, and, defeated, take to the plain. Here there was constant danger in passing small Tibetan villages.

They tried to arrange to go by these settlements at night. But the Tibetans keep fierce mastiffs for house dogs and many times they had to hide quickly as the dogs barked and gave an alarm. Once one of these mastiffs rushed out of a house and badly mauled one of the party. Captain Noel was compelled to shoot the animal. It became increasingly obvious that they would have to ask their way if they were not to blunder around the plain until discovered or their food gave out. So, finding a village at the end of the valley, they walked boldly into it. Not a soul was to be seen in the streets as they went by, though they noted several people peeping at them from behind doors.

The Tibetans, though forbidden by their priests or Lamas to give any information to strangers, are not by nature inhospitable. Fear of punishment in a new life makes them obey their priests but they can be bribed to forget their fears at times. Captain Noel found a man and a woman in the village who befriended him and his party and allowed them to stay for a while in their house. But Noel knew that his presence would be reported to the governor at the nearest military fortress. The problem then was to find the way to the pass into Nepal before the governor's soldiers arrived.

Two small boys told them the way eventually, and they set out hurriedly the next day. The big question in Captain Noel's mind was whether from the top of the pass he would see anything of Mount Everest. When he got there, he met a bitter disappointment. As far as he could see in the direction of Everest, there was nothing but a massive wall of mountains—an entirely new range, unmarked upon any map, and seemingly impassable. The peaks of the mountains farthest away were smothered in clouds. Then, as he still watched, the clouds parted for a dramatic moment to reveal one peak, dominating the others and glowing in the sunset. Quickly he took a compass bearing on it. It was none other than Everest, distant about forty miles.

This was the nearest to Everest any white man had yet approached. But the triumph was offset by the fact that the route appeared an impossible one. A party seeking to climb Everest and starting from the Langpoo pass would have to cross forty miles of mountains before they could get to the foot of Everest.

Captain Noel, however, was determined to try to find some other way to Chomo Lungma, the Goddess Mother of the World. But before he had made much progress, he was met by a party of Tibetan soldiers. They had been sent after him, and after a brush with them, he was compelled to return to India. The journey back took six weeks.

In the meantime a remarkable Scottish doctor, who worked as a research chemist in a London hospital and went mountain climbing in the Himalayas on his vacations, had also been engaged in solving the problem of finding a path to Everest. He was Dr. A. M. Kellas, a shy, quiet, but determined man, who performed outstanding feats of mountain climbing but rarely let anyone know of them. During his vacations he would pack his bags and go off to India, hire a few Sherpas (members of a mountain tribe in Nepal of whom more will be said later) and enjoy himself scaling mountains and exploring. From his talks with the tribesmen of the Himalayas, he discovered details of several passes leading to Everest. He even trained one of the tribesmen to take photographs and sent him off with a camera to get what pictures he could of the world's highest mountain. The man came back with some excellent photos of the glaciers of Mount Everest—the first ever taken.

Dr. Kellas was very secretive about his hobby of mountain climbing, but when Captain Noel returned to India and later London after his expedition into the Forbidden Land, the two met and became fast friends. They compared notes and worked out several routes which would take them to the mountain. They drew up a detailed plan for going together, planning to live off secret caches of food which Dr. Kellas believed he could get dumped along the way by tribesmen. But before this plan could be put into effect, World War I broke and Europe was locked in battle for four long years.

In the meantime both before and immediately after World War I, the Royal Geographical Society in London had been endeavoring to get official permission for a party to go to Mount Everest. Sir Francis Younghusband, who had led the military mission to Lhasa in 1904, was prominent in these efforts and Sir Charles Bell, political resident in Sikkim, undertook the negotiations with the Dalai Lama in the Tibetan capital.

Sir Charles had already won the confidence of the Dalai Lama after many years of work. He was received by the Dalai Lama in his palace at Lhasa in 1920 and it was only after all others had been dismissed and the two were alone together that Sir Charles dared broach the subject of allowing a party of white men to go to the sacred Tibetan mountain, the home of both the gods and the devils of Tibetan religion.

The Dalai Lama, after some discussion, agreed to the project, and so at last the way to Mount Everest was open. The official safe conduct for the party issued by the Dalai Lama read, in part:

"Be it known to Officers and Headmen of Pharijong, Kampa, Tin-kin and Shekar that a party of sahibs will come to the Sacred Mountain Chomo Lungma. . . . You shall render all help and safeguard them. . . . We have requested the Sahibs to keep the laws of the country when they visit Chomo Lungma and not to kill birds and animals as the people will feel very sorry for this. . . . His Holiness, the Dalai Lama, is now in great friendly terms with the Government of India. . . .

"Dispatched on the seventeenth day of the eleventh month of the Iron Bird Year." (Tibetans give names rather than numbers to each year.)

The document was signed with the great Red Seal of the Holy Rulers of Tibet. It had taken sixty-nine year from the time that Everest was discovered to be the world's highest peak to obtain permission to explore it.

CHAPTER THREE

Reconnaissance in Force

THE FIRST FORCE MOBILIZED FOR THE ATtack upon Mount Everest assembled in Darjeeling, India, in the spring of 1921. It would not be an extravagant fancy to call the mountaineers, the surveyors, the cooks, and the porters who made up this expedition, an army. With each succeeding attempt, the feeling grew that the conquest of Everest was not merely a matter of mountaineering but also a form of warfare.

On the one side was Man, with all his skill and cunning, his equipment, his courage, and his tenacity. On the other was the mountain, a massive remote cita-

del, aloof and defiant, rising five and a half miles into
the air.

Nor was this citadel without weapons of its own
with which to throw back the besieging forces of Man.
It seemed able to summon the winds and the snow,
ice, fog, and bitter cold at will to guard against in-
vasion. In the assault on Mount Everest, man must
enter a region where as far as was known no living
thing had ever penetrated and where, it seemed, life
was forbidden to trespass by the laws of Nature.

This first expedition consisted of a handful of Europeans, forty native porters, and a hundred mules. It
was under the command of Lieutenant Colonel C. K.
Howard-Bury and was a joint venture of the Royal
Geographical Society and the Alpine Club. Colonel
Howard-Bury was not a mountaineer but had a wide
knowledge of the Himalayas in which he had traveled
extensively. Dr. Kellas and A. F. R. Wollaston, a veteran mountaineer, were next in command. The others
were Harold Raeburn, an experienced climber who
was to lead the mountain party; Dr. A. Heron, a geologist; Major H. T. Morshead, and Major E. O. Wheeler,
surveyors; G. H. Bullock, a former planter who had
distinguished himself by climbing several peaks in
Africa; and George H. Leigh-Mallory, a teacher at
Charterhouse School, Cambridge, England, and a bril-
liant mountaineer. The expedition's job was to explore
the way to the mountain and seek a route by which it
might be climbed. There was no serious intention of
reaching the summit at this time for there would be
enough to be done in examining the mass of the mountain and searching for a breach in its defences.

Major Morshead with three native surveyors was to
join the party at Kampa Dzong, a Tibetan fortress so
ancient that it cannot be said for certain when it was

first built. He took a different route from the main
party to map more of the unexplored country of Tibet.
Kampa Dzong stands upon the crest of a rock and is so
skillfully constructed that it is not easy to tell from a
distance where the rock ends and the fortress walls
begin. The one seems to be a natural continuation of
the other.

The main expedition set out in two parties from
Darjeeling on May 18 and May 19. Although it is only
one hundred miles in direct line from Darjeeling to
Mount Everest, the actual distance which had to be
traveled was nearer to three hundred, as wide detours
were necessary to avoid passing through a wild
expanse of mountain ranges. Only a few maps of the
country were available and these were by no means
accurate. Where the maps said, for instance, that the
route lay along a river it would be found that there
were several rivers or rather branches of one river.
Which was the main river and which were the
tributaries?

Again, valleys which according to the maps led in
the right direction were found in reality to wind and
twist about, and on one occasion Colonel Howard-
Bury's party was misdirected by some Tibetans who,
despite the letter of the Dalai Lama, were suspicious
of the foreigners. One river marked upon the map as
flowing in one direction, actually flowed in another.
Indeed, a whole book could be written about the expedition's adventures traveling through Tibet, at times
fording fast-flowing, glacial rivers, then crossing a
waste of quicksand, then climbing passes and the
shoulders of lesser mountains, and all the time having
to question the Tibetans about the way to Mount
Everest, the Goddess Mother of the World.

Kampa Dzong was reached by a pass which
mounted to a height of over seventeen thousand feet.

It was here that the first casualty of the war against Mount Everest was sustained. Dr. Kellas had been ill for the past several days, and was so weak he had to be carried in a litter. As he was being brought up the pass that led to Kampa Dzong, he died of dysentery and the exhaustion of the march. He was buried in a simple grave, in view of the topmost peak of Everest, the mountain he had wished for so long to reach. Raeburn also fell ill at Kampa Dzong and had to be sent back with Wollaston. That meant that only two mountaineers, Mallory and Bullock, remained to tackle Everest. But, despite the blow, they were impatient to push on to the mountain whose lure increased the nearer they got to it. On the day following the departure of Raeburn and Wollaston, Mallory and Bullock climbed a barren slope above the place where they had camped the night before to see what lay ahead.

When they had gone up a thousand feet, they turned to look westward in the direction of Everest, and saw the peak of the mountain, glittering in the blue haze of distance. To the left was Makalu, a smaller but imposing summit of which they had been told, though this was the first time either had seen it. Between Makalu and Everest, however, was a black, rocky cone, so near to Everest that Mallory guessed rightly it was part of the main mountain. Everest, then, was not one peak but two, and the new summit came to be known as the South Peak. (It was found later that there was a third summit north of Everest, forming part of its mass, which was called the North Peak.)

Of more immediate concern, however, was the fact that between Kampa Dzong and Everest lay an entirely unknown mountain range called the Gyanka. A way would have to be found through these to get to

Everest and the expedition would have to rely heavily on the Tibetans for directions.

One group of Tibetans, as mentioned, misdirected the party, but most of the people were friendly and willing to help now that their Lamas had said they might aid the foreigners. However there were difficulties.

The Tibetan measure of distance turned out to be a tea cup. A certain place would be stated to be four or five tea cups away, meaning that it would be reached in the time taken to consume four or five cups of tea. For greater journeys the measure was "a long day's travel" or "a short day's travel." But how long was a long day's travel?

The way through the Gyanka mountains, it developed, led along a gorge to the north and then through barren countryside, grim, windswept, and ice-bound. After some days Mallory and Bullock climbed a steep slope to a rocky crest overlooking the gorge to see whether once again they could catch a glimpse of Everest, which must now be much nearer.

All in the direction of the great mountain, however, was misty, or clouded over. The two peered through their field glasses, hoping that these would pierce the clouds. Then, as though torn aside by some invisible hand, the veil of clouds was rent and Everest appeared. The Goddess Mother of the World was not, however, revealed all at once to the first Europeans ever to gaze upon her full size. First, a monstrous edge of black rock, harsh and forbidding, cut through the mists. Then a shimmering gleam betrayed the presence of a glacier as hard as iron. A shoulder thrust up, covered with ice and snow. Finally, the huge head of the mountain appeared, so high above all else around that the two could scarcely believe it.

They looked at each other in silence, and in a minute, the clouds had descended over Everest again, cutting it off from their view. But they had seen enough even at a distance of fifty-seven miles, to gain a much more detailed idea of the problem before them. They had caught sight of a valley running up to the mountain. And they saw that the black mountain before Everest, the North Peak, which they had first glimpsed from Kampa Dzong, was indeed connected with the mother mountain by a huge cliff of snow which they judged to be twenty-seven thousand feet high.

At last, after a month of marching from Darjeeling, the party came to Tingri Dzong, a settlement around another Tibetan fortress, and here it was decided to split up into groups, each with its special duties.

Morshead and Wheeler were to make as complete a survey as possible of the Everest area. Heron was to examine the geology of the ranges about. Wollaston, who had now rejoined the expedition after taking the ailing Raeburn back for medical aid, was to study the plant life of the region. Colonel Howard-Bury, in charge of the whole force, was to see that the needs of all were provided for, and establish a base of operations to which all could return when their tasks were completed. He selected the Kharta Valley on the east side of Mount Everest as a rallying point.

When these plans were made, Mallory and Bullock pushed straight on towards Everest with sixteen porters, a headman or sirdar, and a cook.

Everest, the two learned, is best reached by the Rongbuk Valley; and after some delay they arrived there. Nothing now obscured their view of the mountain. The valley led without interruption up to its foot. To the side lay other peaks, some twenty-six thousand feet high. But compared with the noble stature of Everest, these seemed insignificant. The Goddess Mother was supreme over all.

From the peak there flew a torn flag of cloud and snow, a mile in length, warning of the violence of the winds which men would have to brave to win the summit.

CHAPTER FOUR
Finding the Breach

THE RONGBUK VALLEY MAKES A TWENTY-mile corridor up to the northern face of Mount Everest. For ten miles it forms the channel down which a glacier or river of ice crawls at a rate of a few feet a year. This glacier has its beginning on the steep cliffs of the mountain. Mallory and Bullock knew that by following the glacier they would be brought to the foot of the mountain. But they guessed, so forbidding was the wall at the end of the glacier, that Everest would be too steep to climb at this point.

However, they could not overlook a single chance, and so set off on the following day along the glacier to get to the base of Everest. It looked at first as though the way along the glacier would be easy. But Everest was already beginning to show some of the defenses by which it is guarded. It took not one day but many to explore the northern approach to the mountain. The surface of the glacier was furrowed in places with massive ridges of ice. At other parts pinnacles of ice towered into the air fifty feet above the heads of the explorers. The two found themselves walking through a forest or, perhaps it would be better to say, a city of these glittering towers of ice. They were at times all but lost in them, surounded by beautiful pinnacles, flashing white in the sun; the shadows deep shades of green, blue, and violet. Because Everest is only twenty-eight degrees north of the equator (the same latitude as Tampa, Florida) the sun beats down from directly overhead in summer strong enough to create a mist from the melting of the ice.

In the confined air between the ice towers, the two climbers and their porters were filled with a sense of lassitude so that they had to exert the greatest effort of will to struggle on. They felt an overwhelming desire to sit down and rest among the dazzling peaks. In the end they found that the glacier, which had appeared to be an easy road for them to follow, was best avoided, and took, therefore, to the moraines at its sides. Moraines are collections of stones and boulders stripped off mountains by the slow downward flow of glaciers.

Arriving at last at the end of the Rongbuk Glacier, the suspicion that no route led from there to the crest of Everest was confirmed. Ahead was nothing but a huge ice cliff which would be impossible to scale. But Mallory got one clue to a possible stepping-stone to the mountain. He climbed a lesser peak to one side of the glacier and saw that the eastern slope of Everest was seemingly quite gentle, and came down to a curve ending in another peak. Such a curve connecting two mountain peaks is called a col, and Mallory decided that this particular col, which became known as the North Col, might be the step needed to put the mountaineers on the slopes of Everest itself and on the road to the summit. But first, he wanted to explore what lay nearest to hand. He found another glacier joining the main ice flow, and called it the West Rongbuk Glacier. Many days were spent exploring this but all to no avail. No breach in the walls of Everest was discovered on the West Rongbuk Glacier. The upper end was a jagged, broken mass of ice.

Mallory found another col, however, and struggled up it. From the top he was able to look behind the mountain on the southern side. The sight that met his eyes, though beautiful almost beyond words, was, at the time time, wild and forbidding. Below lay a drop of fifteen hundred feet, down to a new glacier. Mallory thought he might be able to traverse this precipice—that is go down it by crossing at an angle so as to make the descent less steep. But that proved out of the question. As far as he could see there was no way to climb Mount Everest from the south, to which he was now looking. He turned then, after some more exploring, to the North Col, which he had seen earlier.

The first thing to do was to see whether the North Col could be climbed from the Rongbuk Glacier. Examination showed that this would be possible only with the greatest difficulty. The col rose one thousand feet straight up from the glacier floor in a cliff. At its foot lay thousands of tons of snow and ice which had tumbled down the gleaming sides of the col in avalanches. Anyone attempting to climb the col from the glacier would risk being killed by an avalanche thundering down on him.

There was only one thing to do, and that was to find a way to the other side of the North Col in the hope that it might be more easily climbed from there.

At this point Mallory missed a great chance. He caught a glimpse of another glacier, joining the main Rongbuk Glacier a little distance past the North Col. Glaciers, at their "snouts" or ends, dissolve into water, and Mallory noted that only a very little water was coming from this new glacier. He, therefore, concluded that it was but a small one. Although it gave some promise of leading to the rear of the North Col, he judged that it would peter out before getting there. He passed it up. Actually this glacier, known as the East Rongbuk Glacier, does lead to the back of the North Col, but Mallory did not discover this until later. Nor was the glacier as small as Mallory had thought. The reason so little water comes from it is that the sub-tropical sun vaporizes the ice directly without melting it into water. This was something Dr. Kellas, who died in Kampa Dzong, could have told him. As it was, the expedition did not discover this peculiarity of Hima-layan glaciers until later.

To find a way to the back of the North Col called for a detour of some fifty miles due east to the Kharta Valley where it had been arranged that Mallory and Bullock were to meet the other members of the party. Their departure was delayed, however, by news that many of the pictures of Mount Everest and its sur-roundings which Mallory had made were useless. He was not an expert photographer and had put his plates in the camera back to front. The only thing to do was to go back over the ground already explored and shoot some more. Many men might have decided to forget about the pictures. The weather was getting increas-ingly bad. Strong winds and blizzards had started springing up without warning. But Mallory was of such a nature that once he had set himself to a task, he would not be deterred from completing it. Back he went with two porters over the ground he had already explored, and took more pictures of the surroundings of Everest. When this was done he set off with Bul-lock and their porters, in the fury of a blizzard, to the Kharta Valley, fifty miles away.

Here the two with their men entered a paradise which contrasted sharply with the desolate rocks and ice cliffs of Everest. Flowers of many kinds and in a rainbow of colors abounded. The site of the camp in the Kharta Valley was not much over twelve thousand feet and around were pastures of deep grass and groves of tall trees.

It would have been pleasant to rest for a week or so, but Mallory was burning with desire to find a way to climb the North Col, which seemed to him the only method by which Mount Everest could be ascended. He stayed in the valley only long enough to refresh himself and his porters and then set out again. Local guides assured him that by crossing into another valley he would be brought right to the Goddess Mother of the World. This valley seemed to be in quite the wrong direction, but Mallory and his party went with the guides. As it turned out, the new valley, called the Kama Valley, proved a blind alley. But the detour was well worth the making. Beautiful as the Kharta Valley was, the Kama Valley was even more lovely. Flowers and trees of all kinds abounded in its fertile bottom lands. Rising straight out of it on both sides were huge mountains, their peaks clad with snow and ice. The contrast was between lush countryside and an arctic wilderness. At the end of the valley was Everest, but Everest plunging so steeply down that no one could possibly climb it. To one side lay Makalu, only two thousand feet lower than Everest. There was a third peak to be seen, another satellite of Everest, called Lhotse. This was the mountain which became known as the South Peak by the expedition. No white man had ever been in this beautiful valley before. Again the temptation to linger was strong. But again Mallory's determination to find a road up Everest overcame it.

Back he went to the Kharta Valley, and following this to its head, came out, after much hard work occupying many days, to the top of a pass called the Lhakpa La. From here he could look down twelve hundred feet to the East Rongbuk Glacier, which he had missed exploring before. On the other side was the back of the North Col which he fervently hoped would provide the essential stepping-stone to Everest.

It was the work of several days, however, to get to the base of the North Col and set about climbing it. Stores had to be brought up, and the snow in the pass of the Lhakpa La, which was actually the bed of another glacier, was deep. Added to this difficulty, the ice below was full of crevasses or splits, some of them dangerously wide. These had to be jumped, and it was difficult to get the porters to leap them loaded as they were with stores. Yet with encouragement and some urging, the men did their tasks well. One, who proved himself a superman, was found by Mallory lying face down in the snow. He had collapsed carrying, in his eagerness, not one load, but two. His name was Dorji Gompa.

It was decided that only three climbers—Mallory, Bullock, and Wheeler, the surveyor—would attempt to climb the North Col from the East Rongbuk Glacier. To the top it was one thousand feet, but the angle was steep and the walls were ice covered by snow. Mallory knew, however, that if they could not get to the top of the North Col, chances of ever being able to climb Mount Everest would be very slim indeed.

The base was not too difficult, but as the men climbed higher, not going straight up but working at an angle, they came to a part where the snow lay at such a steep pitch as to be almost impassable. Here it was necessary, using ice axes, to cut steps to the top of the col. Five hundred were cut in all, and the party got at last to the summit of the North Col. This was the first real step along the long road to the conquest of Mount Everest.

Once on top of the col, Mallory hoped to be able to climb on some way up the mountain. He felt that he was in condition to climb about two thousand feet. His companions, however, were not in such good shape. Bullock was tired though he was ready to make an effort, forcing himself to walk. Wheeler was game too, but had lost all feeling in his feet—a forerunner of frostbite. Rather than turn back, the three prepared to make one try if only for the honor of being the first to go a little way up Everest.

It was blowing a full gale on the col where the three now stood at a height of twenty-three thousand feet. Even sheltered behind a cliff of ice, the wind tore at their garments, raking through their supposedly windproof jackets with fingers of steel. They stepped out from their shelter to test the full fury of the blast. It was enough to almost knock them off their feet. They had to bend double to stand at all; and snow as hard as bird shot tore at their faces and clouded their goggles. Their feet and legs were lost from sight in a writhing white surf of snow and ice.

The three peered for one terrifying minute at the peak of Everest. Snow was being flung in streamers of white across the face of the mountain, and hurled in sheets from the summit. There was no possibility of going as much as ten feet up the mountain, so violent was the wind. It was as if the Goddess Mother of the World, feeling for the first time the affront of human feet upon her, was bent upon hurling the invaders back. Reluctantly the three returned to the bottom of the col.

But they had achieved a measure of victory. A breach had been found in the walls of Everest. Next time the mountain itself could be stormed.

CHAPTER FIVE

Everest's Secret Weapons

MALLORY, ON HIS RETURN TO LONDON AF-
ter the first Everest reconnaissance expedition, said
that the chances against any given party reaching the
summit of the mountain were fifty to one.

Fifty to one! With odds as long as that, quoted by
an experienced mountaineer, many heads were
wagged; many solemnly proclaimed that Everest
would never be scaled; many announced that human
beings could not survive on its dizzy heights, and
many called the whole venture an exercise for fools.

These critics had a great deal of logic and experience
on their side on which to base such gloomy predic-
tions. The biggest question was: Could men live five
and a half miles up in the air? The only precedent to
point to was the case of three men, H. T. Sivel, J. E.
Croce-Spinelli and Gaston Tissandier, who in 1875
ascended in a balloon five miles above the earth's surface. When they came down two were dead and the
third, Tissandier, was unconscious.

Some years before the first Everest party set off for
the mountain, the Duke of the Abruzzi, an Italian
climber, had ascended to twenty-four thousand and six
hundred feet on one Himalayan peak. This was the
record for mountain climbing at the time. The Italian
had found that he could go no further, being both exhausted and weak from want of air. Everest's peak lay

four thousand four hundred feet higher than the altitude at which the Duke of the Abruzzi had been
driven back. His experience coupled with the death of
the two balloonists was sufficient proof for many that
it would be impossible for anyone to achieve the summit of Mount Everest. If further weight for their argument was needed, it was supplied by the members
of the first Everest expedition themselves.

All had found that strange things happen to them
when they got three miles above sea level. A little exertion tired them completely. They became readily ir-
ritated. Some suffered from violent headaches. Others
experienced severe pain and swelling of the throat. The
tissues in the back of the mouth and nostrils became
dry and stiff like thin paper. At one time or another all
suffered these painful symptoms. But other symptoms
had been experienced which were more serious. There
was a marked falling off both of the power to reason
and the will to undertake anything unpleasant. Boiling
a pan of water became a major problem. Cutting steps
in ice, a normal mountaineering chore, and by no
means heavy work on lower mountains, became, on
Everest, as much as a man could manage. If a climber
rested for a few minutes, he could hardly bring himself
to move again. It took enormous will power to make
one more step, even though survival might depend
on it.

Vision also was affected. One of the experienced
Sherpa porters in going up the pass which led to the
East Rongbuk Glacier had such difficulty in seeing
where to put his feet that he misjudged his step and
went rolling down the snowy slope.

These symptoms were not entirely new to such
veteran mountaineers as Bullock, Mallory and Wollaston. What surprised and dismayed them, however,
was that the symptoms were so marked in climbing

around Mount Everest and did not go away when the men descended to lower levels, as was the case on lesser mountains. Indeed, Mallory discovered that the headaches, the exhaustion, the sapping of both mental and physical strength which overtook him on the slopes of Everest seemed to increase rather than abate when he turned around and descended.

The Tibetans have their own explanation for all these reactions. They say they are the work of devils, for they believe that both gods and devils live on their great mountains. If a block of ice or a rock falls upon a man, it is the work of a devil. If he breaks a leg, a devil has reached up from the ground and tripped him. To offset the influence of these devils, the Tibetans erect mounds of stones, called chortens, wherever such an accident occurs and decorate them with strips of rag. Then when they pass, always on the right-hand side, they say a prayer to Buddha for preservation. The prayer is always the same one—"Om mani padme hum," which means "Hail, Jewel of the Lotus Flower."

Among their other beliefs is that a frightful being called a Sukpa lives in the snowy wastes of Everest and other mountains in the Himalayan range. The Sukpa, or Abominable Snowman, is a huge hairy beast like a man or an ape who seizes human beings as his prey. He can jump great distances when chasing anyone, and has a stiff tail on which he can sit down. When he has caught someone, he contents himself with biting off his victim's nose, and the tips of his fingers and toes. This would suggest that some of the fiercesomeness of the Sukpa is attributable to frostbite, for frostbite first affects the extremities—nose, fingers, toes, and ears. Because the Sukpa is so hairy, the best chance of getting away from him, the Tibetans believe, is to run downhill. His long hair then falls into his eyes and he cannot see to continue the chase.

Neither gods nor devils, however, were acceptable explanations to the members of the expedition for this altitude sickness. They correctly blamed lack of oxygen. There were two schools of thought as to how the difficulty could be met.

One school, to which Mallory inclined, believed that it would be possible to acclimatize to the lack of oxygen, if the ascent were taken slowly. The theory was that if a man spent say a week at sixteen thousand feet above sea level, then went on to twenty thousand feet, staying there two or three days, his system would adjust to the lack of oxygen. In this way it would be possible to get to the top of Everest though the ascent would naturally be prolonged.

Mallory, a man with both a poetic and a scientific bent of mind, had studied the problem of breathing in the rarefied air of mountains for some time, and had developed a formula of his own for use in mountain climbing. He discovered that if the drawing in of a breath was timed exactly to the lifting of a foot from the ground, and the breath was exhaled completely as the foot went down, he did not suffer so badly from altitude sickness. At greater heights, he practised a more rigorous method, taking two breaths to each step. His breathing plan seemed to work for him. Its real virtue seemed to be in making breathing a conscious effort. Mallory found that when he forgot about breathing for a while and breathed naturally, he did not get enough air and suffered from mountain sickness.

Others found that they were aided in overcoming altitude sickness—that is, headache and lassitude from lack of oxygen—if they smoked cigarettes. The secret lay, apparently, not in the cigarette smoke, but in the fact that in drawing it in, breathing was deliberate and somewhat deeper than normal.

One school, then, held that men could acclimatize themselves in time to such an extent that they could live five and a half miles or even more above sea level. Another, however, believed this either impossible, or said the process would be so lengthy that months would be needed to get to the top of Everest. These argued that the climbers should carry oxygen cylinders with them, fitted with breathing tubes which would enable them to draw on the oxygen when needed.

The arguments whether oxygen should be carried or not were lengthy and inconclusive. At that time oxygen equipment was elaborate and cumbersome. A major question was whether the climbers could carry the heavy cylinders to such an enormous height. In the end it was decided that on future expeditions, some would climb with oxygen, some without. That would put the matter to the test.

Other difficulties besides altitude sickness were uncovered by the first Everest expedition.

On mountains in the Alps, for instance, it was known that if the sun shone after a snow storm, it would melt the top layer of snow. During the night, this top layer would freeze again and present on the following day a firm surface to climb on. The same process held true on Everest only up to twenty-three thousand feet. But beyond that, however much the sun melted the snow surface, and however cold was the night which followed, the snow remained powdery and threatened to peel off from steep slopes in avalanches. Scattered thinly upon rocks, such snow was slippery and dangerous to walk on. Where the snow lay deeper on more level surfaces, it would not support the weight of a man. Many times the climbers were forced to flounder thigh deep through snow while their lungs cried out for air.

An explanation of this peculiarity of Everest's higher

snowfields is that the snow is vaporized by the sun without turning to water. That which is not vaporized remains in its granular form. This strange state of affairs confronted Mallory and Bullock and their porters in climbing up the Kharta Valley to the pass which led to the East Rongbuk Glacier. They found themselves walking in an oppressive, steaming atmosphere, so thick that they could see no more than a few feet ahead. And yet all around lay snow and hanging glaciers of glittering ice. It was something like being in a Turkish bath which was contained, miraculously, in a refrigerator.

A final difficulty in the way of climbing Everest lay in the monsoon. Monsoon is the name given by the Arabs (who are among the world's finest sailors) to a seasonal wind which blows across the Arabian Sea—six months from the northeast and six months from the southwest. The Arabic word "mausin" or "mawsim" from which monsoon comes means season. By extension, monsoon came to mean the southwesterly wind which sweeps across India from the Indian Ocean. It commences to blow in the beginning of June, and continues on through September.

When this wind, laden with the moisture picked up during its passage across some four thousand miles of ocean, reaches the Himalayas, it is forced upward by the mountains, the moisture freezes, and heavy falls of snow result. Thus, during the monsoon period, the Himalayas, and with them Everest, are blanketed with snow, rendering climbing exceedingly difficult and dangerous. The 1921 expedition carried out its work during the monsoon.

It was decided that in future, attempts on the mountain would be made before the monsoon, starting in March or April. That would give the climbers a period of some weeks during which the mountain could be expected to be fairly free from snow.

Although the monsoon itself is not necessarily a violent wind, when it forces its way through the Himalayan peaks, its velocity is enormously increased. Winds of a hundred miles an hour and more accompany the monsoon on Everest, and no man, even in the peak of condition, can fight such a fury.

When the 1921 expedition returned to England, four months remained in which to get everything organized for the first real attempt to climb the mountain.

The assault on Everest took on the aspect of a race— a struggle against the elements, with a time limit set, in which all might be won or lost.

CHAPTER SIX
The First Attack

LATE IN MARCH OF 1922 THE FIRST ATTEMPT upon the summit of Mount Everest was ready to be launched—again from Darjeeling in India. It is necessary to list only partially the equipment and personnel gathered together to realize the determination and planning which lay behind the effort. Nothing however small which would contribute to success was omitted. There were ice axes and crampons (spikes fastened to the sole of the boot to aid in climbing ice-covered slopes), ladders and ropes, lanterns, windproof clothing and tents, special boots and goggles, food of an almost endless variety, cameras, cylinders of oxygen, fuel and stoves, ponies, mules, surveyors, mountaineers, doctors, porters, and medicines. These were the weapons to be used against Everest.

Against them, the mountain could summon a terrible arsenal of its own. But Everest was unable to devise new weapons and add to her defenses. If man could prove himself cunning and brave and tireless enough, he must eventually conquer.

Some who had taken part in the reconnaissance of 1921 were in the first assault party, but the expedition contained many new members. It was under the command of Brigadier General C. G. Bruce, chosen not only because of his extensive mountaineering in the Himalayas, but also because he had a deep knowledge of the mountain people of Nepal among whom porters were to be recruited. General Bruce had served thirty years with Gurkha regiments (the Gurkhas are Hindus from Nepal and make excellent soldiers), so was obviously the man who could get the best out of the porters of the expedition. He had proposed climbing Mount Everest as early as 1893.

Second in command was Lieutenant Colonel E. L. Strutt, a seasoned Alpine climber. Neither, however, was expected to take an active part in the actual climb towards the peak. That job was to be entrusted to younger men. Of these, the first was George Leigh-Mallory, who had been with the reconnaissance of 1921. With him was Captain George Finch, who was to have joined the first expedition, but had not been able to do so because of illness. Next came Major E. F. Norton, an artillery officer and mountain climber who had made a reputation for himself in India for his skill at pig-sticking. Norton was a man of many talents, his hobbies including painting and bird-watching. In pursuit of his interest in bird-watching, he had done a great deal of climbing in the Alps. He was a man who was never flurried, and prided himself on his punctuality. Dr. Howard Somervell, another climber, was a surgeon as well and a great humanitarian. On his return after the attack on Everest, he was so struck by the poverty and the prevalence of disease among the people of India that he decided to stay there and help them as a medical missionary.

Then there were Dr. Wakefield, an Englishman with a medical practice in Canada which he left to take part in the Everest adventure; Captain Geoffrey Bruce, a cousin of General Bruce; C. G. Crawford, of the Indian Civil Service, and Major Morshead, who had been a member of the 1921 venture.

Dr. T. G. Longstaff was appointed naturalist and official medical officer of the expedition, and Captain Noel, who had made the secret trip to Tibet described earlier, was the photographer. Dr. Longstaff was himself a great mountain climber, and at one time held the record for the highest peak reached—Mount Trisul, twenty-three thousand four hundred and six feet, which he climbed in 1907. The final European member of the expedition was Captain C. G. Morris, an officer in a Gurkha regiment, who was to aid with transportation and supervision of the porters.

On March 26 the start was made from Darjeeling, but the oxygen cylinders had not arrived and Finch and Crawford waited behind for these. By April 11 the expedition had reached Kampa Dzong, buffeted by hurricanes on high mountain passes on their way, for the Tibetan winter was not yet over. They followed much the same route as the previous expedition, but met worse weather. By April 30—a little more than a

month after the start from Darjeeling—they were at
the Rongbuk Monastery at the head of the Rongbuk
Valley.

General Bruce and his companion called on the
Lama at the monastery to pay their respects. They
found him a man of striking character, with a face so
quick to express feeling, to change from laughing to
solemnity, from anxiety to reassurance that he might
have commanded, elsewhere, the highest fees as an
actor. This expressive face of the Lama of Rongbuk
Monastery did not surprise his flock, however. They
believed him the reincarnation of the god Chongray-
say—a god who has nine heads and therefore nine
faces!

It would be wrong to think of the Lama, however,
as anything but a devout, sincere and in many respects
a noble man. He had great dignity and courtesy, and
asked the members of the party not to injure any living thing in the valley. They promised they would
abide by his wishes and he confessed his curiosity as to
why they should come so great a distance to climb
Mount Everest, or Chomo Lungma as he called it.

The question took General Bruce aback for a while.
He had had difficulty in giving a satisfactory answer
when asked the same thing by many of his own people
in England. But he told the Lama that there were certain Englishmen who worshiped mountains, and the
expedition was, in a sense, a pilgrimage to the Goddess
Mother of the World. The reply was satisfactory and
was not strictly untrue, for certainly the love of mountains, characteristic of mountaineers, is a form of wor-
ship.

General Bruce took advantage of the interview to
excuse himself from drinking Tibetan tea, a concoction
beloved of Tibetans who consume it in copious
amounts, but not suited to the taste of others. Basically

it is a green tea in which lumps of butter, frequently rancid, are melted. Other ingredients include salt and nitre. General Bruce said that although devoted to butter, he had taken a vow not to touch it during his present pilgrimage. Thereafter he was excused from drinking Tibetan tea though the others were forced to partake of large quantities as a matter of courtesy.

The plan for the ascent of Everest was based on the establishing of a series of camps up the mountain's sides. The reason for these camps was simple enough. It was quite out of the question that a party of climbers starting at the top of the North Col, the stepping-stone to Everest, would be able in the course of one day to scramble all the way to the top and come back down by dark. Not only would the distance be too great but there would be no chance for the climbers to acclimatize themselves to the rarer air and the decreased atmospheric pressure as they mounted upward. Then too, it was necessary to have some kind of shelter in which the climbers could wait out a blizzard on the mountain without having to return all the way to the bottom.

Everest, it was agreed, would have to be climbed in stages, with success depending on how good the weather might be before the monsoon, and also on how high the last camp could be placed upon the mountain. The climbers themselves could not carry all the equipment needed to establish their string of camps up the mountain side and then be in shape to make the final climb to the peak. Porters were needed, and of those engaged, the Sherpas proved to be the finest. These are the Tibetans who live in the high valleys of Nepal near the southern side of Everest. They are mountain people by birth, accustomed to heavy labor at high altitudes, cheerful, courageous, and hardy. They played an enormously important part in

the conquest of Everest. Without the help of such
porters, no attempt on the mountain would have been
possible. Yet it is strange that in all the time they have
lived in the neighborhood of Everest and other giant
peaks around, they made no attempt on their own to
scale these mountains. Perhaps they could see no point
in undertaking what to them would be nothing but
hard work. Mountain climbing is not a sport among
the Sherpas.

The expedition established its base camp at the
snout of the main Rongbuk Glacier, at an altitude of
sixteen thousand eight hundred feet. Here most of the
Tibetan porters quit and had to be paid off, but there
was still a body of perhaps fifty or sixty others hired
from Nepal who stayed to help establish the camps.

A reconnaissance party, under Strutt and including
Norton, Longstaff, and Morshead, was sent up the
East Rongbuk Glacier to survey sites for camps and in
a matter of days these had been established as far as
the foot of the North Col—the cliff of ice, one thousand
feet high, which had to be climbed to get onto the
northeast slope of Everest. The camps were not set up
without casualties. Longsaff became ill from altitude
sickness. There was trouble with the porters, resulting
in delays. But some more Sherpas from Nepal joined
the party, traveling over lonely mountain passes to get
to the base camp. Many brought their wives and these
in turn brought their children, some of them under a
year old. The mountain tots did not seem to suffer
from altitude at all, and their mothers were able to
carry loads with all the stamina shown by the men.

In all, three camps were established on the East
Rongbuk Glacier. Camp One was about three hours'
walk from the base camp; Camp Two was four hours
up the glacier from Camp One; and Camp Three at
the foot of the North Col had an altitude of twenty-

one thousand feet and was four hours from Camp
Two. Cooks were stationed at each camp to supply
food to those making their way up and down the
glacier and all in all the system of camps up to the
North Col worked well enough.

Mallory and Somervell, once the glacier camps were
established, were the first sent to find a way to the top
of the North Col and if possible establish Camp Four
there. They were to be accompanied by two porters to
carry gear but one of them, after a night in the freezing wilderness at the foot of the North Col, was too ill
to go on. The two mountaineers then set out with one
porter to get to the top of the North Col and find a
site for a further camp.

The cliff had, of course, been climbed the year before, but the aspect which it presented now was very
different. The previous year it had been largely covered with the snow brought by the monsoon. Now the
snow had congealed into pillars and sheets of ice,
gleaming hard and blue in the sunlight. In places this
ice was split by deep fissures. One fissure which had
to be crossed was seventy feet deep—a menacing
green cavern, set like a death trap in the perilous path
to the top. It was too wide to be jumped and the only
way across was a natural bridge of snow which had
formed within the fissure. Gingerly one of the mountaineers stepped onto this to test whether it would
hold his weight. He was roped to his companion. He
walked a foot or two out onto the arch of snow over
the green depths. The snow crunched under his feet
at every step. But the bridge held. Would it be strong
enough to support porters carrying loads of twenty
pounds and more?

Mallory and Somervell could take no chances on
that. They reinforced the span by stamping more snow
down upon it, and stretched ropes across the crevasse

fastened to wooden pegs for the porters to hold on to. It was no easy task to get to the top of the North Col. Some two thousand steps had to be either cut in hard ice or stamped in the snow before they arrived at the lip of the ice cliff and, hauling themselves up, could claim to have climbed the first step of Everest.

Now the wind blew so hard that it nearly knocked them off their feet. Their porter could come no further, and they had had to leave him to rest on a shelf below the top of the cliff. Despite the wind, the two were determined that they would that very day walk along the cliff to where it joined the north ridge of Everest to make sure that the way was clear for the climbing party. It was lucky that they did. They had gone only a few yards before they were stopped by a huge crevasse, about fifteen feet across, which was quite impossible to negotiate without a ladder. They had to detour to find a way around this. Then they found two further crevasses which had to be crossed. Over one there was an ice bridge to take them to the other side. The other was comparatively small though deep and they jumped it. Now they were on the slopes of Everest proper—the first men to stand there. But there was a fee to be paid for their achievement. Both, after their exertions, began to suffer badly from headache, a symptom of altitude sickness. It was late in the afternoon and they had to get back to camp before dark.

Mallory and Somervell took one final look around at the mountain which they had come such a distance to climb and returned to the camp at the base of the North Col. When they got there, they slept for thirteen or more hours, too exhausted to move. Mallory was unable to eat anything, though Somervell ate heartily enough. They had intended to pitch a tent on the top of the North Col the next day. But both were so tired that they rested three days before any further effort could be made. In any case, they would need porters to carry stores and tents for the camp on the top of the ice cliff.

Even resting was difficult at a height of twenty-one thousand feet, with a keen subzero wind blowing night and day. The only place they could get warm was in their sleeping bags.

Yet they made themselves as comfortable as they might, and passed the three days, waiting for the porters to arrive, making side trips and reading to each other. Mallory had brought with him two volumes, one Robert Bridges' anthology, *The Spirit of Man*, and the other a book of Shakespeare, which included the tragedies *King Lear* and *Hamlet*.

With the wind moaning over the wilderness of ice and snow, Everest towering above, and the blue-green ice cliff directly in front of their tent, Mallory opened his Shakespeare for what comfort he could find there. The first lines his eyes fell upon were the words of Hamlet, on seeing the ghost of his father, "Angels and Ministers of Grace defend us."

They seemed very appropriate at the time.

CHAPTER SEVEN
Triumph and Disaster

CAMP FOUR WAS PLACED ON THE TOP OF the North Col by May 20, and on that day Mallory, Norton, Somervell and Morshead started with four

porters up the north ridge of Everest to establish Camp
Five. This was the jump-off camp for the summit. It
was hoped that it could be placed at a height of
twenty-six thousand feet. That would leave three
thousand feet to be climbed to the peak. In the Alps a
mountaineer could climb about one thousand five
hundred feet in an hour. At the higher altitude on
Everest, it was presumed that his rate of climb would
be reduced to one thousand feet an hour. With only
three thousand feet to ascend to the peak from the last
camp there would be ample time, it was thought, to
get to the top and come down again before dark.

But as it turned out Camp Five had to be placed a
thousand feet lower than was planned. There were a
number of reasons. The cold proved so severe, as the
party climbed up the north ridge of Everest, that they
had to stop to put on extra clothing. A minor tragedy
overtook Norton at this juncture. He was sitting on
the mountain side with his knapsack containing extra
clothing on his knees. Mallory, some distance above,
pulled the rope linking the two of them to clear it.
The knapsack tumbled from Norton's lap. It went
rolling down the slope of the mountain—first slowly,
then picking up speed, hopped from boulder to
boulder and ledge to ledge, until eventually with one
great bound, it disappeared from sight headed for the
Rongbuk Glacier a mile below.

Then the wind started to blow—only a breeze at
first, but a breeze so cold as to penetrate the thickest
clothing. There was every sign that it would turn into
a full blizzard. Again, no place could be seen higher
up on the bleak mountain suitable for pitching a tent.
It would be useless to climb to twenty-six thousand
feet only to have to come back in search of a level or
sheltered spot to put up the two tents which the

porters were carrying. Finally, there was the problem of seeing that the porters got back safely to Camp Four before dark.

All in all, it seemed wisest to pitch the tents at twenty-five thousand feet. Even so, it took two hours to find a place to erect them. The north ridge of Mount Everest is not precipitous. Indeed, the mountain would present no great problems for climbers if it were not so high and so exposed to an evil variety of weather. But the slope is steep nonetheless with hardly a level spot in all its length. A small ledge was found on which one tent could be pitched. The other had to be erected on a sloping slab of stone at the lower end of which a little platform of stones was built to provide some sort of level ground. It was the sorriest of sites in which to pass the night, in a tent, particularly at a height of more than four and a half miles above sea level. This was believed the highest any human being had ever slept in the history of the world. The climbers had to melt snow to obtain water. Because of the low atmospheric pressure, the water boiled at a temperature so low that a finger could be put into it without hurt.

The porters were sent back and the four men went to bed nursing their boots under their heads to prevent their footwear freezing. For warmth they slept in pairs, two in each tent, in double sleeping bags. On the way up, one of Norton's ears had become frost-bitten, so he was compelled to sleep on one side all night to protect his ear, with sharp stones sticking into his flesh. Mallory discovered that three finger tips of his right hand hurt as if they were badly bruised—a symptom of frostbite. He put this down to cutting ice steps during the day, when, the better to handle his ice axe, he had taken a leather glove off his right hand

and put on a wool one instead. Morshead had suffered
acutely from the cold during the day. It was suspected
that his toes were frostbitten. All in all it is surprising
that any of the four got any sleep that night in their
tiny tents which clung to the steep frozen sides of
Everest.

They were up the following morning at 6:30. After
breakfast the four roped themselves together, adjusted
their boots, shook their aching joints and set off. They
had not had enough sleep to get them through a day
of light office work. Ahead lay a grueling climb of four
thousand feet to the top of a frozen mountain.

They had not gone more than a few paces before
Morshead said he could go no further. The cold of
the previous day had worn him out and he was not acclimatized to the altitude. He did not want to keep the
others back, or prove a burden by collapsing when
they got higher up All were anxious about his condition. It is no small decision to leave an exhausted man
alone in a camp on a deserted mountain side, but
Morshead assured them he could look after himself
though he was incapable of climbing further. So they
left him to return to the camp and pressed on to the
summit.

Pressed in this case is exactly the right word. It was
a matter not of walking or climbing though the ground
was not hard to travel on. It was rather a question of
pressing with the full resources of mind and body to
lift up each foot and put it down again and to pull
the scanty and freezing air into their lungs. Breathing
had to be consciously attended to. There was no such
thing as breathing naturally. Each lungful of air had
to be deliberately drawn in and as deliberately ex-
pelled. Somervell stated he had to take five breaths to
a step at this altitude. Only twenty or thirty minutes

could be spent at a time in climbing. Then the three had to halt for four or five to get the strength to go on again.

There was fresh snow on the mountain which had fallen during the night; not a great deal of it, just a few inches. But it was sufficient to slow the men's progress further. The climbers found that they were making not one thousand feet an hour as they hoped, but only four hundred excluding the time spent resting. Their pace was getting slower the higher they went. At four hundred feet an hour it would take ten hours to get to the summit of Everest even if they were not held back by some unexpected obstacle. Obviously there was no sense any longer trying to get to the top. Mallory looked at the aneroid which measured their distance above sea level. It told them that they were at twenty-six thousand nine hundred and eighty-five feet. (The point they reached was triangulated later and proved to be twenty-six thousand seven hundred feet.) The peak lay only a little over two thousand feet higher, up what appeared an easy slope, though with a hard scramble at the end. In the thin air it seemed but the shortest distance away. Yet cold mathematics told them that they had no hope at all of reaching it; that to keep on would be suicide, for their remaining reserves of strength would be exhausted and they would not be able to get down again.

They had established, however, a world record for climbing. They had set the record without the use of oxygen. And they had done this after spending the night in two miserable little tents at twenty-five thousand feet; something that no one had ever done before.

These were great achievements and yet such is the effect of altitude upon the mind that the men did not feel at all pleased with their performance. They were not even particularly interested in their surroundings. The mountaineer normally delights in the eagle view he obtains from a height. But the three men paid only scant attention to the magnificent vista that lay below them. A few yards would have taken them to the crest of the northeast shoulder of Everest, and they could have looked over into hitherto unseen territory. They weren't interested. Now that they realized that they could not reach the top, the only matter which concerned them was getting down. They did not want merely to get down to Camp Five, two thousand feet below, where Morshead was waiting; they wanted to get right down to Camp Four on the North Col.

So they found a place offering a mite of shelter and ate a lunch of candy, raisins and prunes. The food was extremely difficult to swallow. Their mouths were dry from the exertion of climbing and from the freezing air which they were breathing, and they had not a drop of water with them to slake their thirst. Nor was there any prospect of finding any. One of the three—by tacit agreement his name was never revealed—produced a small flask of brandy. He was carrying it despite medical opinion that alcohol would be very injurious if taken in the rarified atmosphere on the heights of Everest. Nonetheless each took a sip, and found himself remarkably refreshed. Mallory later said, wryly, that in view of medical opinion on the subject, the brandy must definitely have been non-alcoholic.

Then the three started back down. They were weary, perhaps closer to exhaustion than they realized. Certainly they were in that dangerous state when with mind and body thoroughly tired, instincts are less sharp, limbs are not quite under control and consciousness is dulled. Everest was waiting for just such an occasion.

They found Morshead at Camp Five in much worse condition than when they had left him. He was suffering from severe frostbite though still able to walk. It was decided that he must be got down to the North Col that day, where he could receive some attention.

All went well for a while until the four men, roped together, came to a snow slope, the lower edge of which led to a precipitous drop of thousands of feet to the East Rongbuk Glacier. The slope would not have provided exceptional difficulty for a party of fresh men but for climbers in their condition, it was a distinctly dangerous place to cross. The main hazard lay not so much in the steepness of the slope, but in the fact that the snow was fresh. Granular and soft, they might readily slip on it and be hurled over the precipice to death on the glacier. They started out carefully and all went well for a while.

Then, suddenly, the third man on the rope slipped. Normally he could have been held by the fourth man, but he was moving and fell also. The two dragged the second man off his feet. All three commenced sliding helplessly down towards the edge of the precipice. Mallory, in the lead, sensed, without looking around, that something had happened behind him. He drove his ice axe into the snow and took a turn of the rope around the head. Then, holding the rope with one hand, he threw all his weight on the ice axe, pressing it into the snow to make it hold. There was just the slimmest chance that he could alone take the weight of the three men. Otherwise all would be killed. The rope tightened and jerked at the axe head, slipped for an agonizing second and then, when all seemed lost, held firm. Norton, Somervell, and Morshead were stopped within a few feet of the precipice. The only

immediate comment out of them was made by one
(unnamed in Mallory's account) who denounced the
fact that he would have to climb up all the distance he
had slipped down.

This, however, was not the end of their troubles that
day. Morshead, though he had borne up well and
without complaint, was rapidly approaching complete
exhaustion. No stop to rest was possible for it was
beginning to get dark. Furthermore, a rest of two or
three minutes would not do Morshead much good.
And a longer rest in the biting cold might prove fatal
to a man in his condition. They had to go on. For
most of the way, Norton or one of the others supported Morshead around the waist, stumbling with
him down the treacherous mountainside. Darkness
came. The four men could see each other only as dim
shapes looming in the murk. They looked forward,
anxiously, to getting to the camp on the North Col
where they were sure they could get hot drinks, make
themselves warm, and rest. They had had nothing to
drink all day but a sip or two of brandy.

At last they came to the North Col. The camp itself
was pitched on a ledge on the side of the ice cliff and
they had yet to make their way across the top to it.
This was frightful work. Pinacles and walls of ice rose
on either side of them like a glittering maze. They had
a candle lantern, but frequently lost their way.
Finally, they recognized a fifteen foot wall of ice,
from the top of which they had jumped previously
to clear a crevasse at the bottom.

There was only one thing to do now and that was
jump again, weary though they were. None of them
liked the idea. They were not sure that, jumping in
the dark, they would land safely. There was the hor-
rible thought that instead of landing on the ice below

they might plunge instead into the huge fissure at the bottom of the wall. But jump they did, though Morshead had to be lowered on a rope. They all made it without mishap.

It still took some time to get to the camp on the ledge below. The lantern flickered out. A guide rope to lower them to the ledge where the camp was pitched had become lost in the snow. It looked as if they would have to go down in the dark without it. One false step might bring a fall of a thousand feet to the East Rongbuk Glacier. But at last someone found the guide rope. There was a cheer from the others and they all got safely to the camp.

The first thing now was to get something hot to drink to ease their parched throats. They were hungry, but would have to take liquid food first, for their mouths were so dry they could not swallow anything solid.

Then came the final blow.

The porters had removed the cooking pots in which the four climbers had hoped to melt snow to make tea.

But Norton had an idea—ice cream! He said if they opened a can of strawberry jam and another of condensed milk and mixed both up with snow, they would have strawberry ice cream. The jam was frozen and so was the condensed milk. But they managed to break the ingredients up enough to mix them together with some snow, and swallow a few mouthfuls. Then they rolled wearily into their sleeping bags for a much-needed rest. But what with frostbite, exhaustion, and the effects of their unique strawberry ice cream on empty stomachs they got very little sleep.

There was only one blessing and they were thankful for it. The wind did not blow that night.

CHAPTER EIGHT

"English Air"

THE FIRST ATTEMPT TO CLIMB EVEREST HAD failed. The second under the leadership of Captain George Finch, with Geoffrey Bruce as his companion, and a Gurkha (Nepalese) soldier Tejbir Bura as porter was to use oxygen. The Tibetan and Sherpa porters called this "English air." They knew nothing of the properties of oxygen, but concluded that since the English had a zest for climbing mountains, it was the air they breathed in their homeland which produced it. They reasoned that the Englishmen had brought over a supply of "English air" to help them to the top of the world's highest mountain.

The climbing plan, except for the use of oxygen, was the same as that for the first assault. A camp was to be pitched at twenty-six thousand feet, and after a night there, Finch and Bruce would set off for the peak. Tejbir would carry additional cylinders of oxygen as high as he could, leave them, and come back. These containers would form a reserve for the climbers when they descended.

Again, however, lack of a level place to pitch a tent combined with the fury of the wind, prevented a camp being established at twenty-six thousand feet. Finch had to settle for twenty-five thousand five hundred. But a dozen or so porters had been able to get up that far, and so there were plenty of supplies at this jump-off camp. When the tent was up, all returned to the North Col, leaving Bruce, Finch, and Tejbir behind. The porters got back in the nick of time. What had been a bitter cold wind turned into a full gale. The tent at the jump-off camp had been pitched on the crest of the northeast ridge of Everest, for there was no level place on the leeward side (the side away from the wind) to erect it. On that side Everest drops thousands of feet into a steep precipice.

When the gale came up, the wind shrieking as if a legion of demons was roaming the sides of the mountain, the three had to fight for their lives. Huddled inside the tiny canvas shelter, they were in constant danger of being blown off the precipice to the glacier below.

The fury of the blasts was such that time and again the ground sheet of the tent, together with the three men sitting upon it, was lifted into the air. They had to use all their strength to keep the tent fastened to the ground. Every little hole, every crevice and crack in the canvas was blocked up. But still the particles of snow came in, driven by the force of the wind through the tent fabric itself. Soon all were covered with a coating of fine snow, which clung to their eyelashes and beards, making them look, in the dim light of the tent, like specters.

Sleep was impossible in the nightmare night that followed. The weary hours were spent in keeping the tent down. They could not talk to each other over the roaring and shrieking of the wind. At one point a savage gust tore away the lacing of the tent door. With hands aching from cold, they gripped the flaps together, ripping their fingernails, until the lacing was repaired. Again, a stone flung by the wind like a cannon shot, hurled through the skin of the tent leaving a large hole. Frantic repairs were made before the air pressure caused by the wind streaming through this hole ripped the whole structure to shreds.

All the next day the gale continued, relaxing only for a few minutes at a time. In these lulls, one or another of the party went outside to tighten the guy lines which held the tent to the ground and this alone prevented it being flung off the precipice. A little wall of stones was built to form a windbreak. The three managed, somehow, to get a spirit stove going and made tea and cooked a meal. The gale lessened a little after midday, giving the men a chance, if they wished to take it, to retreat to the North Col. But they stayed grimly where they were.

That evening a party of porters from the North Col Camp arrived to see if all were well. They brought hot beef tea in vacuum flasks.

During the night, however, the effect of the ordeal began to show. Bruce and Tejbir were nearing exhaustion. Finch felt a numbing cold creeping slowly over his limbs. A sleepless eight or nine hours lay ahead. And on the morrow, they must try to climb to the peak for they could not wait another day on the mountain side.

In the hope that it would help, one of the oxygen cylinders was hooked up to breathing tubes and the men took a few tentative breaths. Warmth and strength flowed miraculously into their numbed muscles. Tejbir commenced smiling again. Bruce, whose breath had been short and shallow and whose face was drawn, revived right away. Finch fixed up a gadget whereby all during the night they could get breaths of oxygen from the cylinder. As a result they slept well and awoke the next morning thoroughly refreshed.

Everest, for a while, decided to relax its counterattack on the invaders. The gale died down and was replaced by a gentle though bitter wind. It took Bruce and Tejbir an hour, holding their boots over a candle, to thaw them out sufficiently to put them on. They had neglected to put them in their sleeping bags to prevent them freezing. At last all was ready. Bruce and Finch, carrying cameras, vacuum flasks and their oxygen cylinders, were each toting a load of forty pounds. Tejbir, whose job it was to carry extra ogygen cylinders, was carrying about fifty pounds but would not be required to go all the way to the peak.

The three roped up and set off at a steady pace, with the summit of Everest shining in the morning sun like a shield of gold above them. Progress was good for some time and then the wind began to freshen a little. It was by no means a gale, but a steady current of freezing air which bit through the stoutest clothing. Tejbir suffered the most, for although he had plenty of clothing it was mostly woolen, and wool will not repel the wind. He tried his very best with fine courage, but at twenty-six thousand feet he sank, with hardly a sound, to the ground. He could go no further.

Bruce and Finch relieved him of his spare oxygen cylinders, got him rested, put some spirit back in him, and sent him on down to the tent to await their return. They watched him on his way to see he was safe. Then they untied the rope which connected them, deciding that since the slope was easy, there was no need for it and went on. They climbed steadily, the peak coming nearer and nearer, so that it seemed that in quite a short while they would be there.

Everest, however, was not going to surrender so easily. The wind which had already proved too much for the valiant Gurkha now increased. It commenced to whimper and howl across the lonely mountain, striking at the two dwarf figures that crawled slowly up

the northeast ridge. Eventually it forced them to leave
the ridge and stumble along the side or north face of
the mountain. Here the ground was cloaked with pow-
dered snow. The rocks which form the main body of
Everest are flat like thick tiles, and overlap each other,
sloping outward and downwards. Finch and Bruce
found that climbing on these slabs was like walking
along a sloping roof of rough shingles, covered with ice
or snow, with the wind trying to pitch them off.

In places the slabs gave way to deep snow which
was powdery and could not be trusted. These snow
patches had to be crossed with the greatest caution.
The two remained unroped, however, because in that
way they could climb more rapidly, although if one
slipped there was no possibility of the other saving
him.

Now and then they had to halt to replace an empty
oxygen cylinder with a full one—for they were carrying the extra cylinders which Tejbir had brought as
far as he could. It was bitterly cold work doing this,
standing still in the icy wind fumbling with valves and
nuts. But each time they dumped an empty cylinder,
they were relieved of five pounds weight. They would
throw it away cheerfully and watch as it went clang-
ing down the mountainside, ringing like a gong, until
at last it disappeared from sight.

After leaving the ridge to get out of the wind, Finch
and Bruce had not been making much height, having
reached only twenty-seven thousand feet. Now they
decided it would be better to start climbing towards
the ridge again.

They set themselves gamely to the task, Finch leading with Bruce, the less experienced, coming along behind. Suddenly Bruce cried out. Finch turned and saw
him struggling with his breathing set. Bruce's oxygen
supply had been cut off. This was the crisis both had

dreaded. Medical opinion was that if a man's oxygen was cut off at such a height he would die in a few minutes because his system would not be adjusted to breathing the rarefied air.

Finch raced to Bruce who was stumbling towards him. He quickly cut Bruce in on his own oxygen while he cleared the blockage in Bruce's apparatus. Fingers fumbled in the cold air and it seemed an interminable time before Bruce's tubes could be checked and a repair effected. But eventually it was done. The two grinned at each other and went on.

Their barometer now read twenty-seven thousand three hundred feet—higher than any man had climbed before. All around was a vast wilderness of mountain peaks. These thrust upwards from the distant earth—pillars of ice and stone and snow, piercing the clouds as if seeking to touch the sky themselves. Flashes of gold and silver came from them where they caught the sun. In the shadows were darker hues of green and blue and purple and over this jewelled scene, veils of mist stole so that the colors constantly shifted, silver turning to blue and gold to green as the light changed.

Finch and Bruce, watching this enchanting scene, never before glimpsed by human beings—unknown perhaps even to eagles and the most high flying of birds—realized with a flood of excitement that there was something different about these mountain peaks. They were all below their feet. Everest alone looked down upon them—like a mother upon her sons.

The summit of the Goddess Mother of the World was a bare half mile away. It was so close that in the clear air they could pick out what looked like individual stones on the base of the peak. It seemed that with but a little more work, perhaps an hour or two of climbing, they would be there, standing on the ridgepole of the roof of the world. Half a mile away

. . . a scant seventeen hundred feet above them . . .
and yet they knew that they could not reach it. To get
as high as they were had used all the strength they
had available for climbing. To spend any more effort
would mean they could not return. If they went up as
little as a few hundred feet more, they would have to
be prepared to die. The temptation to go on, to risk
paying the price of death for the prize of being the
first to reach the peak of Everest, was almost irresistible. But Finch decided against it. They had already had trouble with the oxygen tanks. They could
afford no more. They must return now, content with
having set a record mark, and leave the final triumph
for another day.

So they turned their backs upon the summit and set
off down the mountain again. There were no troubles
during their descent. They found Tejbir asleep in his
tent, and porters coming towards them. Safely back
at Camp Three below the North Col they ate an enormous dinner. Bruce had severe frostbite in the soles
of his feet. Finch also had four patches of frostbite on
his feet, for the cold had been so intense it had penetrated the half inch sole of his climbing boots and two
pairs of heavy woolen socks.

So the second attempt to reach the summit failed.
But oxygen had showed its value. Bruce, taking his
last view of the peak as they came down, summed up
the feelings of both. "Just wait," he said. "We'll get
you yet."

The relative success of the attempt by Bruce and
Finch to climb Everest with oxygen, resulted in the
decision that another oxygen attempt would be made
that year.

There was some difficulty in selecting the climbers,
for all were now suffering from frostbite or exposure
or both. Bruce's feet were in such bad condition that

he had to be sent back to Darjeeling. He was incapable of walking. Finch thought he would be all
right, but his feet troubled him badly and he found
himself very weak, and eventually had to admit that
he couldn't make another climb. He also went back
to Darjeeling.

Morshead's frostbitten fingers and toes were in a
serious state and it was obvious that he could only
save them by getting down to a lower elevation as
soon as possible. Norton's feet, though he complained
only of bruises, were also frostbitten, but, more
serious, his heart had been affected by his strenuous
efforts in high altitudes. He had to be ruled out. Mallory's heart had also given him some trouble. He
developed a murmur in it. One finger of his right hand
was black with frostbite at the end. Dr. Longstaff
warned him that it would be very sensitive to cold
and he might lose it if he exposed the finger again.

This he was prepared to take a chance on, but his
heart was another matter. Mallory had taken up mountain climbing in his youth because he had a weak
heart, and believed the exercise would strengthen it.
That his heart was now showing symptoms of strain
worried him. However, after a few days rest, the murmur in his heart disappeared, though any unusual
exercise set his pulses racing and his heart beating
very rapidly. But he decided that he was fit enough to
make another attempt to the summit.

Four climbers, eventually, were pronounced fit
enough for the third assault upon Everest. They were
Mallory, Somervell, Wakefield, and Crawford. The
weather, however, was now showing signs of breaking
up. Every morning was clouded until nine or ten, and
there were flurries of hail and snow. Two nights were
spent at Camp One, with heavy snow each night. Then
the weather cleared a little and in one day the party

reached Camp Three. Here they found the stores buried in deep snow. The tents had been struck, and had to be erected again. The snow was dangerously deep around, but next day the sun shone brightly, much of the snow melted and the whole prospect looked far more encouraging.

It was again decided to try to pitch Camp Five—the jump-off camp for the summit—at twenty-six thousand feet. And it was agreed that far more stores than had been available to previous climbers would be needed, particularly food. This meant, with spare oxygen cylinders to carry as well, that a great number of porters would have to be used. And this called for delays, for the climbers had not only to escort the porters up but also back down. It was an established policy that porters were always to have an experienced climber with them coming back down the mountain lest they get into difficulties.

The climbers would not start using oxygen until they got to twenty-five thousand feet. That would save on the number of cylinders which had to be carried.

This then was the plan—a plan which had fair prospects of success.

The start was to be made on June 7.

CHAPTER NINE
Avalanche

JUNE 7, 1922, BROKE BRIGHT AND CLEAR over Mount Everest. The sun shining strongly out of

a sky of deepest blue, turned the ice pinnacles of the
East Rongbuk Glacier into a fairy city of glittering,
sparkling towers. There was no wind, and every ex-
pectation that the good weather would continue for
the whole day, giving Mallory and his party plenty of
time to get to Camp Four on the North Col.

There had been a sharp frost during the night, and
it was hoped that this would have frozen the surface
of the heavy snow to a hard crust on which to walk.
But when, after breakfast, the party set out to the
North Col, that thousand foot cliff of ice and snow
which formed the stepping-stone to the sides of
Everest, they found that though the surface of the
snow was frozen, it would not support the weight
of a man.

The climbers sank several inches into it. There
would be some very hard going before the ice cliff
could be climbed. And there would be, Mallory
realized, a real danger of avalanches. An avalanche is
the sudden falling away of a huge body of snow,
bringing with it blocks of ice and boulders weighing
many tons. It is the accident which is most feared and
most guarded against by mountaineers. When there is
any danger of such a catastrophe, the snow must be
carefully tested by trenching—that is cutting into it—
to see whether it is secure or inclined to slip.

Because of the fear of avalanche and because the
snow lay so deep upon the steep sides of the North
Col, it was decided that Mallory, Somervell and
Crawford (Wakefield was to remain at Camp Three
as supply officer) would go ahead, testing the snow
and stamping a way in it for the porters who were
to follow. The climbers would have to go ahead
anyway, for the porters laden with supplies would not

be able to fight their way through the knee-deep snow without a path being made for them.

The most likely place for an avalanche to occur was in the final two hundred feet from the top of the ice cliff. The porters of whom there were fourteen, were roped together in three parties—four, five, and four. The three climbers were also roped together—the last of the porters being on their rope.

All went well for the first few hundred feet. There was not a sound to be heard except the stamping of feet in the snow and the quick drawing in and expelling of breath as the men bent to their work. The snow tested out very well. Mallory trenched in several parts where an avalanche was likely to occur, but the snow remained solid. It seemed stuck to the wall of hard blue ice below. It was not even necessary to cut steps to ensure a safe footing.

Upward the climbers and porters struggled, four little groups of men, like flies crawling on an enormous glistening white wall. They arrived at the spot near the top where an avalanche, if one occurred at all, was most likely to start. Overhead was a huge boulder of ice, gleaming green and blue in the surrounding white. It was not pleasant passing under this, but the snow seemed so firm that now all thoughts of avalanche had been dismissed.

Then the silence was broken by a heavy, muffled explosion. The snow around commenced to wrinkle up, and the seventeen men started sliding slowly but helplessly down the face of the ice cliff. They were caught, just when all seemed safe, in an avalanche.

Mallory spun himself outwards so that he would fall upon his back rather than on his face. With the instinct born of many years of training, he started flailing his hands in the air as if swimming upon his back.

This is the drill for anyone caught in an avalanche. A wave of snow engulfed him, Somervell, and Crawford. He was completely buried, but conscious of sliding down the ice cliff at an increasing rate. The pressure on his body increased as more snow tumbled on him. And then, quite suddenly, all was quiet. He struggled for a minute or two and found himself on top of the snow, having as a result of "swimming" brought himself to the surface. He looked quickly around. Somervell and Crawford were a few yards away, both unhurt. The porter on their rope was also safe. About fifty yards below a group of four porters on another rope were standing. But there was no sign of the other two groups, one of five men and the other of four. They had been buried by the tons of avalanching snow and ice.

The three Britons hurried down to where the porters were standing and found a cliff of bare ice with a snow-filled crevasse at the base. Beyond was a pile of snow flung down during the avalanche. It was all too plain what had happened. The two missing groups of porters had been dragged over this ice cliff, which was about forty feet high, and buried.

A rope led down into the crevasse and Mallory, Crawford, and Somervell started digging the snow out with their ice axes, and shoveling it aside with their hands. They came to a pair of boots, dug more and faster and pulled out one porter. He was dead. The rope led further into the fissure. They dug again, not pausing for a minute, and came across a second man. He was so tightly wedged in that the oxygen tanks had to be cut off his back before he could be brought out. Though he had been buried for forty minutes, he was still alive. The rope led further down. Two other men were below. Mallory and the others dug again as the minutes went by, but could not get to them. As fast as they flung the snow aside, more fell in. At last they had to give up. The two men could not have survived burial so long, and there were others in the snow pile to the side of the crevasse who must be got out.

Four of these were dead. They had fallen forty feet or more onto a lip of ice as hard as a rock and been broken there. In all, seven were killed in the avalanche while seven survived, not including the three Britons.

The latter were still concerned about the two bodies in the crevasse. They would gladly have dug them out but the other porters said it would be better to leave them there. They did not seem especially disturbed by the loss of their seven companions, some of whom were relatives. They believed that the men had been sacrificed to the anger of the gods of Everest. Their time had come and so they had died, and there was no reason for either grief or regret.

Mallory, Somervell, and Crawford, however, felt very deeply about the accident. Time and again they asked themselves whether it had been any fault of theirs that the men had died. Yet every test to which they had submitted the snow indicated that all was safe. They had no way whatever of knowing that an avalanche would occur. They re-examined the place where it had happened and found that the snow had not split where they had been standing but some distance above. They concluded that higher up the snow was not rooted so firmly to the ice and the movement of the porters climbing up had been enough to pull it away.

The survivors returned to the base camp, defeated. Everest, on a windless, sunlit day, had in one minute snuffed out the lives of seven men who had trespassed on her sides.

CHAPTER TEN
A Round for Everest

EIGHT MEN HAD DIED—SEVEN PORTERS AND
Dr. Kellas—in the assaults upon Mount Everest. A
handful had climbed to within what would, on any
other mountain, have been easy reach of the summit.
But the Goddess Mother of the World was still unconquered. And the members of the Mount Everest
Committee of the Royal Geographical Society and
the Alpine Club were determined that another attack
on the mountain would be made.

Again the delicate negotiations to obtain permission
to climb had to be conducted with the Dalai Lama
who once more acceded to the request. Again the complicated task of getting together stores and transportation, porters and equipment of all kinds had to be undertaken. And again the personnel had to be selected.

The start of the new attempt was set for the spring
of 1924. General Bruce was once more in command,
and of the members of the 1922 expedition, several
were willing to make another try. Among them were
Mallory, Somervell, Norton, and Geoffrey Bruce. New
men were N. E. Odell, who obtained leave from a job
in Persia to join the expedition as climber and geologist; Bentley Beetham, a schoolmaster by profession
and a mountaineer by inclination; Hazard, who earned
his living as an engineer but found his relaxation

mountain climbing, and Andrew Irvine, an under-
graduate at Oxford University, twenty-two years old,
of magnificent physique and some experience in
Alpine climbing. General Bruce referred to Irvine as
"the experiment." He had not as much mountain
experience as the others. But his youth, his strength
and his enthusiasm were all in his favor. It remained
to be seen whether these would avail him on the
windswept ridges of Everest.

E. O. Shebbeare, of the Indian Forest Department,
joined the party in India as transport officer and Major
R. W. G. Hingston of the Indian Medical Service as
medical officer. Captain Noel, who did a great deal
toward financing the expedition by arranging to sell
the movie rights, came as photographer.

The long journey over Tibet to the base camp on
the Rongbuk Glacier—now so familiar to many of the
climbers—brought only one incident and that an un-
fortunate one. In the bitter Tibetan winds General
Bruce collapsed with a bout of malaria, so severe that
he had to return to Darjeeling. Norton took over the
command. The party arrived at their old base camp in
the Rongbuk Glacier on April 29, with all their plans
prepared in advance for establishing a series of camps
up the mountain, with the last, Camp Seven, at
twenty-seven thousand feet or so.

That would leave but two thousand feet to be
climbed to the summit by climbers who would have
rested for a night in Camp Seven and so would be
reasonably fresh. With eight climbers available, it was
planned to make four attempts to reach the summit
with two climbers in each try. Two efforts would be
made with oxygen and two without. Stores had been
labeled for the different camps, so that all would be
correctly distributed at the stops up the mountainside.
The whole attack had been planned to the tiniest de-

tail—even to the climbers bringing books with them to read to take their minds off their troubles in the cold thin air of Everest's heights.

But it was not to be as easy as that. No sooner had the men arrived at their old base camp than they were caught in a snowstorm. It was colder than even the veterans of Everest could remember. Snow or no snow, the schedule had to be kept strictly, and all worked through the storm, blinded by the driving flakes, to get a hundred and fifty porters ready to start up the glacier with their stores for the different camps.

Camps One, Two, and Three were established, but the weather was so foul that at Camp Two one party of porters could go no further.

They were told they might dump their stores there to be carried up later. This was the right thing to say to relieve exhausted men. But unfortunately, all the porters, exhausted or not, decided to dump their stores at the same spot and go no further. So all the careful plans for keeping separate the stores for each camp came to nothing. Supplies marked for camps high up on the mountain were mixed up with those to be used on the glacier. High altitude stores were broken into to relieve purely temporary emergencies. The whole transport system ground to a standstill .

Alternative plans then had to be formed. Some stores had to be repacked. Spirit had to be put into the porters to take them up to the further camps, and all this, difficult enough with experienced help and in kindly weather, was enormously complicated by incessant snowstorms. It was not only the cold and the driving snow which added to the burden of the job. The altitude slowed the men down and made even so small a task as lighting a pipe an operation consuming several minutes.

Eventually, some kind of order was restored, and a porter service organized, though many of the Tibetan porters left because of the weather. The next step was to examine the thousand-foot-high North Col and see whether it was in a condition to climb. Camp Four was again to be established on the North Col. It was always necessary to have a camp there so climbers could rest after scaling the ice cliff or before descending to the East Rongbuk Glacier below.

The weather deteriorated so badly that it was quite impossible to inspect the North Col, let alone climb it. Living in tents on the glacier with the wind howling around them, the thermometer falling to thirty-nine degrees below the freezing point, with food ill-cooked and ill-served, affected the morale of the whole party. Even before they had fairly started on their attempt on Mount Everest, the spirits of all were low. Some kind of a boost was needed. The porters—including those who had served on previous expeditions—were convinced that the mountain gods and devils were intent upon driving the expedition back. They recalled the fate of the seven porters killed two years before and grew despondent. They felt that if they made any effort to climb the slopes of the Goddess Mother of the World, they would be killed too. Two did die; one of frostbite and the other of a hemorrhage in the brain, bringing Everest's death toll to ten. In this atmosphere of defeatism, Captain Noel suggested that all return to the Rongbuk monastery and ask for the blessing of the Lama on their endeavor.

The Lama agreed to bless the expedition, though warning one or two of its members that the gods of the mountain were showing their disapproval of the attempts to climb it. When his blessing had been conferred on everybody—Europeans as well as Tibetans and Sherpas from Nepal—they turned again to the attack.

Strangely, the very next day the skies cleared, and the sun shone brightly. The camps up the glacier to the North Col were soon occupied. Norton, Mallory, Somervell, Odell, and one Sherpa, Lhakpa Tsering, set out to find a way to the top of the North Col. The North Col is really part of a hanging glacier, or a waterfall which is frozen solid. Like all glaciers, it moves at a very slow but none the less measurable pace. Consequently its appearance from year to year is quite different. The place where the avalanche had killed the seven porters two years before was still visible. But the rest of the face was now covered with a series of horizontal crevasses in the ice. One of these led to the hollowed out chute where the avalanche had fallen two years before. It was decided to follow the lower lip of this crevasse into the chute and then climb upwards to gain the top of the ice cliff.

A whole chapter could be written about this particular maneuver. At one point the climbers had to descend one side of a crevasse in the ice and then scale the sheer opposite side for the gap across was too big to be jumped. Again they had to ascend several hundred feet up a wall of ice so steep that snow would just rest on it. A slip here would mean death on ice boulders hundreds of feet below. But they blazed the way to the top and Camp Four was established by porters who were able, on the following days, to follow this trail up the North Col.

Then the weather, which in 1922 had been sunny and fairly windless at this time of the year, turned foul again. Hazard was in Camp Four with twelve porters. He decided, because of the wind, to get

down to the glacier below before night, and set out
with his porters to do so. Four of them, however,
without informing Hazard who was ahead leading the
way, lost their nerve and decided to stay the night in
Camp Four.

This was a very serious decision indeed. The four
men were not experienced climbers. They could not
get down on their own. They had food but not much,
for a load of eatables had been dropped in the ascent
of the ice cliff. When it was discovered that they had
stayed behind, it was too late to bring them down the
same day. But a rescue party was organized to get
them on the morrow.

Somervell, Mallory, and Norton formed the rescue
team. Both Somervell and Mallory were suffering
from altitude throat—a swelling of the throat membrane and muscles—which can become so severe as
to make it almost impossible to breathe. They were
racked with coughs every few minutes, but climbed
the most difficult parts of the ice cliff in fifty minutes.
One of the marooned porters, watching them coming
up, was seated on a shelf of ice overhead. He called
out that another of the men had badly frostbitten
hands and another frostbitten toes. But he believed
all would be able to come down under their own
power, and he went off to get them.

Somervell walked carefully out on to a snow slope
so steep that he could, standing up, lean his elbow
against the side of it. Mallory and Norton tied the end
of a rope around his waist and the other to a pinnacle
of ice so that he would be held if he fell. But when
Somervell got as far as the rope would allow him, he
was still thirty feet from the men on the ice shelf.
They would have to make that crossing on their own.

The first two got over without incident. But the last

two stood close together, so that the snow on the steep
slope under them could not stand the weight. It commenced to avalanche. The men were dragged relentlessly, unable to help themselves, towards the edge of
a cliff which dropped several hundred feet to the
glacier, expecting to be hurled to their death. Then,
only a few feet from the edge of the precipice, they
were brought to a halt by the snow piling up before
them. But both were so panic-stricken they could do
nothing but stand where they were, looking at the
chasm a few yards from their feet.

Somervell shouted to them to sit down. Then, taking
the end of the rope in his hand, and reaching out as
far as he could, he grabbed one by the collar and
pulled him back. He chaffed at them good-naturedly
for putting him to all this extra work, and succeeded
in restoring their nerve so that one was able to laugh.
Soon both were pulled back to safety. They passed,
floundering along the rope, to the other two climbers.
Then Somervell came back over the steep slope, walking as calmly as if he were crossing a street.

All then returned to the lower camps on the glacier
to await an improvement in the weather, for wind and
snow now had their way on Everest, and the North
Col camp was untenable. Beetham had come down
with crippling sciatica and though he put his whole
will into overcoming the condition, was not capable
of doing any climbing. Somervell and Mallory were
suffering acutely with their throats and very weakened
by their part in the rescue of the four porters. Two
men had died. And so far no one had put a foot on
Mount Everest proper.

The first round in 1924 went to Everest by a clear
decision. But the climbers were not yet beaten. They
would be back to fight again when they had rested.

CHAPTER ELEVEN

Higher than Ever

AFTER A SPELL TO RECOVER STRENGTH AT the lower camps, the climbers started out again. Camp Five was placed at something over twenty-five thousand feet by Mallory and Bruce in weather so cruel that it was an ordeal to move as much as a hundred yards up the frozen sides of the mountain. A party of fifteen porters was all that was available out of a force of fifty-five to carry the loads needed to establish the camp. Of these only eight could make the climb from Camp Four on the North Col to Camp Five. These porters, all Sherpas, earned the name of "Tigers" for their stout-hearted work in carrying loads to high altitudes in the bitter weather. A medal was struck later in London with a tiger's head on one side. It was given to any porter who carried a load to twenty-six thousand feet on Everest, and became a coveted decoration among the men.

When Camp Five was erected on June 1, over thirty days after the expedition's arrival at the old base camp on the Rongbuk Glacier, Mallory and Bruce had to go back to the North Col. They had been unable to persuade their porters to go further to establish Camp Six, which was to be set at twenty-seven thousand feet, and was to be the jump-off camp for the summit.

Now it was up to Norton and Somervell to try to get Camp Six in place and also make an attempt at

reaching the top of the mountain. Their climb was to
be made without oxygen. They had with them six
porters, but during the night which they spent at
Camp Five, two of the porters were hurt by falling
stones. One suffered a head wound, the other a nasty
gash across his knee cap. On the following morning
only three porters could be persuaded to climb further
—one of them being the man whose knee was badly
hurt. His name was Semchumbi. The others were so
exhausted by the biting wind and the lower atmospheric pressure that they could hardly be persuaded to cook breakfast for themselves.

Four and a half hours of climbing, every breath
drawn painfully and with great labor, brought them to
twenty-six thousand eight hundred feet. Here Semchumbi, climbing with a wounded knee and carrying
a load of twenty pounds on his back, could go no
farther. Camp Six had to be pitched at a considerably
lower altitude than was planned. The porters were
then sent back to the North Col with a note saying
that they were to be fed on the best available as a re-
ward for their fine performance, and returned to base
camp on the Rongbuk Glacier for a well-earned rest.
It was not necessary for either Norton or Somervell to
escort them down because the camp below was in full
sight, and the way plainly marked.

After a fairly comfortable night at Camp Six, Norton
and Somervell prepared to make an attempt to reach
the peak of Everest. The day was calm—the first really
good climbing weather the expedition had experienced, although so late in the year the monsoon was
expected at any time. The two set off in bright sun,
though the cold was intense.

They had on layers of windproof garments. Their
hands were sheathed in thick mittens. They wore hats
to protect their heads from the direct rays of the sun,

goggles to guard their eyes from the infra-red rays which can cause snow blindness, and their faces were shielded from the bite of the wind by leather masks.

Norton found so little snow lying around that he occasionally removed his goggles to see better, replacing them only when they came to snow patches.

In one hour's climbing the two men reached a big band of yellow rock which cuts across Everest and is a thousand feet high. This band is a readily distinguishable feature of the mountain even from a great distance away. They found it consisted of a series of broad ledges, and they were able to walk up it at an angle quite readily. The cold, however, began to tell upon them. Temperatures of fifty degrees below zero have been recorded on the heights of Everest.

Norton found himself trembling so badly that he took his pulse, thinking that he was coming down with a bout of malaria. To his surprise he found his pulse was only about sixty-four, twenty above his normal beat. At twenty-seven thousand feet he began to have trouble with his eyes. He had periods of double vision —seeing things twice and thus being uncertain where he should put his feet. He thought he was in the beginning stages of snow blindness, but Somervell assured him his trouble was merely the result of there not being sufficient oxygen in the air.

The strain of their exertion, of the lack of oxygen and the lowered atmospheric pressure now began to have a marked effect. Neither climber could go more than a dozen paces without having to stop and pant for breath doubled over with elbows on knees. Somervell's throat, which had recovered somewhat during the rest period at the glacier camps, began to swell again, aggravated by sucking in fast gulps of the frigid, thin, dry air. He was taking as many as ten breaths for every step. By midday the two had reached the top of the yellow band of rock. Ahead lay a huge gully or scoop in the mountain (couloir is the mountaineer's word for it) which would have to be negotiated. Beyond that was the base of the summit.

But Somervell could go no further. His throat was threatening to close up on him completely, and he could scarcely breathe. He urged Norton to keep on, saying he would stay where he was until he returned. There was just a chance that Norton could make the summit alone.

Norton then climbed on by himself. He edged cautiously around two buttresses into the gully which had to be crossed to get below the summit. The gully he found filled with loose snow, the worst kind for climbing on. Alone, with no one to help him in case of a slip, he went into this, sinking at times to his waist. Beyond the gully the going got steadily worse. Now instead of slabs of stone to walk on there were only the tiniest of ledges; nothing but an inch or two of rock pitching outward and downward at an acute angle. Below was a sheer drop of several thousand feet.

Foot by foot, each step carefully calculated, with death the penalty for making a mistake, he edged up. Four hundred feet or more would bring him to the final pyramid and what looked like an easy, safe climb to the summit of Everest. Then only two hundred and fifty feet. He inched upwards on rocks so narrow that he was supported only by his fingers and toes. His vision got worse. Everything had a double outline. He could not be quite sure where to put his feet down. But he pressed on.

At last he came to a place but two hundred feet from the base of the summit. Less than nine hundred feet above him was the top of Everest. He looked at his watch and knew in that moment that Everest had beaten him. It was one o'clock. He was climbing at a rate of only one hundred feet an hour and was so exhausted he could go no faster. That meant that it would take nine hours, barring mishaps, to get to the top. It would be dark before he was half way there and no man could climb on Everest in the dark and live. There was nothing for it but to turn back.

So, he turned. At the time, so dulled was his mind by exertion and by lack of oxygen that he felt no disappointment at his failure. He was conscious of little more than a relief that the ordeal of the upward climb was over. He rejoined Somervell and the two struggled down to Camp Four on the North Col. They were so weak that they took several hours to get to the camp. At one point Somervell found that he could not breathe. Norton was ahead and did not notice that his companion had stopped, and was struggling for air. He turned when he heard Somervell give a loud agonized cough. A great quantity of blood and membrane came out of his mouth slopping down the front of his tunic. The cough probably saved Somervell's life, by making it possible for him to breathe again.

Eventually they got to the North Col camp. Here the others were waiting for them with hot soup and congratulations for having broken all mountain climbing records. Norton had reached twenty-eight thousand one hundred and twenty-six feet on his lone climb. Mallory was full of plans for another attempt by himself and Irvine with oxygen. They would carry the oxygen up to Camp Six and only use it from there on to the peak.

That night Norton found there was a penalty to pay for climbing so high on Everest. He was awakened by severe pains in his eyes. Next morning he was snowblind. Despite the fact that he could not see, Norton did what he could to help Mallory and Irvine by telling them of conditions they might expect to meet and places to avoid. Then he shook hands with them before they set out for the jump-off camp. He could not see them, but had to content himself with imagining them climbing up the mountain side.

Once Mallory and Irvine had left, Norton decided that if he stayed at Camp Four he would be a burden on the men there, and despite his blindness he must climb down the thousand-foot wall of the North Col to the camp below. Hingston, the medical officer, examined his eyes and said nothing could be done for them for the moment. Norton's sight would return in time but there was no way to speed the process. Hingston, however, with the aid of Hazard and two porters, volunteered to get Norton down the ice cliff.

Hingston was not an experienced mountaineer. But he conducted himself with all the calm of a veteran. Norton put on crampons—steel spikes fitted to the sole of the boots like ice skates. Hingston commenced down the ice cliff, carefully putting Norton's feet in the niches in the ice for him. Hazard stood above with a rope around Norton's waist to save him if he slipped. Step by step they went down a steep gully with a straight drop of hundreds of feet to boulders of ice below. Then they had to cross the gully to the lip of a crevasse. They climbed across the lip, Norton incapable of helping himself very much and the others placing his feet for him. It was slow, nerve-racking work. To the blinded man each unusual sound suggested an impending accident; each slip the potential start of an avalanche. Yet he kept his nerve and with the aid of his companions finally reached the bottom.

Arriving on the glacier Norton had to be carried over the rough boulders and through the ridges of ice to the safety of Camp Three. Next day his sight commenced to return and in two days he had completely recovered the use of his eyes. Then he waited anxiously with the others to hear how Mallory and Irvine had fared.

CHAPTER TWELVE

Climb to Eternity

MALLORY AND IRVINE LEFT THE NORTH Col on the morning of June 6, for their assault on the summit of Everest. They had eight porters with them, carrying supplies and spare oxygen cylinders because they had changed their plans and decided to use oxygen all the way during their ascent. They were to spend the night of the 6th with four porters at Camp Five, four returning to the North Col. The next day they were to climb to Camp Six with the remaining porters. These were to be sent back when the camp was reached. The night of June 7 was to be spent by Mallory and Irvine alone at Camp Six and on the 8th they were to start for the summit, returning the same afternoon.

Odell, the geologist, also a skilled climber, was to provide support by advancing first to Camp Five when they had left it, and then going up to Camp Six to await their return from the peak.

All went as planned. Mallory sent a note to Odell from Camp Five saying there was no wind and the weather looked hopeful. It was a comforting message for Mallory was not thought to be fully fit for the ordeal. He had not completely recovered from his

strenuous part in the rescue of the porters from the
North Col camp earlier. Irvine too was suffering when
he set out, from altitude throat, which seemed to be
aggravated by the use of oxygen. He was not, as has
been said before, a fully experienced climber. But he
was the only one available who knew how to fix the
oxygen apparatus if anything went wrong. At twenty-
two he had all the vigor of youth and had caught from
Mallory the same fire to set foot upon the top of
Everest. With Mallory the conquest of the mountain
had become a mission akin almost to the finding of the
legendary Holy Grail by the knights of King Arthur's
court. He thought of little else, turning his eyes constantly towards the peak when in the camps below;
depressed and miserable when the weather forbade
climbing, buoyed up with hope when a break appeared
in the leaden skies and a bleak sun shone through.

Before he set off on his attempt to reach the summit,
he told the others that he expected no mercy from
Everest. Nor was he going to give any himself. He had
been forced to turn his back upon the peak before.
This time, things would be different.

He and Irvine reached Camp Six on June 7 as
planned, and sent back the remaining porters with a
note to Odell who now advanced to Camp Five. The
note said Mallory had left a compass, and asked Odell
to find it for him. The weather was perfect, he reported, and he and Irvine believed they could reach
the summit carrying only two cylinders of oxygen. But
these, at twenty-seven thousand feet, still represented
a tremendous load.

Odell, at Camp Five, two thousand feet lower down
the mountain, sent his own porters back, for they were
feeling the effect of the altitude. He spent the night
alone in the camp, but not disturbed by his solitude.
His interest in geology was such that he intended the

next day to take a stroll along the face of the mountain, examining rock specimens. It is a sharp comment on how differently this expedition viewed Everest that a man would go rock hunting at heights which climbers in 1922 had only just been able to reach.

The next day, June 8, dawned clear enough, though banks of mists formed to the west and swept in majestic, ghostly silence across the face of Everest. Odell packed some provisions in a rucksack and started at about eight o'clock towards Camp Six. He believed that Mallory and Irvine must by now be somewhere near the peak. Mallory was always an early starter, and would not delay, both because of his eagerness to reach the summit and because of the necessity for getting down the same day to the camp on the North Col.

Odell was in no particular hurry. He stopped now and then in his climb to the jump-off camp to pick up rocks, to shelter a while from the cold wind behind ledges and to take in the view. At twenty-six thousand feet he found a crag about a hundred feet high. He could have walked around the base of this but to test his climbing abilities at this altitude decided instead to scale it.

When he reached the top he looked towards the ridge leading up to the summit of Everest. There was a mist between him and the peak of the mountain, but suddenly this cleared to reveal the whole summit and part of the ridge approaching it. On this ridge there are two "rock steps," one below the other and a con-'siderable distance apart. They appear from a distance like humps in the profile of the mountain.

Straining to see if he could spot Mallory and Irvine, he saw a tiny figure moving up a snow slope near the second rock step. Another figure followed. They could be none other than the two climbers. They were going strong.

As Odell watched, the first figure climbed to the top of the rock step. He could not be sure whether the second joined the first for the mist closed in again.

That was the last glimpse ever obtained of Mallory and Irvine. Odell, unsuspecting that any tragedy lay ahead, looked at his watch and noted that it was 12:50 P.M. He was surprised that the two climbers should have taken so long to reach the second step where he had seen them. They should, according to his calculations, have already reached the summit whereas they were still some hundreds of feet from it, though showing, at that distance, no signs of acute fatigue. According to Mallory's schedule, he should have reached the point at which Odell saw him almost five hours earlier. Odell guessed they had had some difficulty with their oxygen apparatus that morning and so had been forced to make a dangerously late start.

Odell continued on his way up the mountain and arrived at Camp Six, which the climbers had left that morning, at two in the afternoon. The wind started to freshen, and he put the load of provisions which he had brought for them in the tent. Scattered around were some oxygen cylinders and parts of the breathing apparatus, and he concluded from this that they had definitely had some trouble with their oxygen. Either that or Irvine the night before had been doing some work to improve the design. He liked to work with tools and was a skilled mechanic.

The weather now worsened. It was snowing without any signs of a letup, and Odell decided that since Camp Six was designed to house only two men, he had better retreat to Camp Four on the North Col. Mallory had said in his note of the previous day that he and Irvine would return to the North Col after their attempt. Odell left the compass that Mallory had asked about in a conspicuous place in the tiny tent and went down to Camp Four, where he filled up on hot soup, for he had spent two days now on the mountain, alone most of the time.

Nobody was particularly perturbed that night about the fate of Mallory and Irvine. It was reasoned that since they had apparently set out late for the summit, they would be late getting back. They might have had to stop to spend the night at one of the higher camps. Still Odell and Hazard, who was also at Camp Four, kept a watch on the mountain for lights or distress flares. But nothing was seen other than the filtered moonlight bathing the cold, impassive face of Everest.

The following morning, through field glasses, Odell and Hazard scrutinized the two camps—Five and Six —on the mountainside for any sign of life. With mounting anxiety Odell decided to go up on a search. He arranged a code of signals with Hazard, who was to stay below, by which they could communicate with each other. Sleeping bags laid out in the form of a letter T would mean "no trace." Other signals would mean that the climbers had been found and were well, or that they had been found and were injured or dead. In case Odell was delayed on the mountain after dark, he and Hazard would communicate with flashlights.

Two porters were persuaded to join Odell in the search. A bitter crosswind was sweeping over Everest from the west. The Sherpas faltered constantly, and it took three and a quarter hours to get to Camp Five. Anxiously Odell pulled aside the flaps of the two little tents. They were empty except for those supplies which he had left there the previous day. These had not been disturbed. Now the only hope that Mallory and Irvine had survived their climb lay in Camp Six, two thousand feet higher up. If they had not made that camp, but had been forced to spend the night unprotected on the bitter slopes of Everest, they could not possibly have lived. Even if they were able to get enough oxygen to keep them alive, the bitter cold would certainly have killed them.

It was now 3:30 in the afternoon, too late to try to climb to Camp Six that day. The wind was blowing with gale force. The snow scurried in writhing streamers of white across the mountain. There was nothing for it but spend the night in Camp Five and set out the following morning, June 10, for Camp Six to see if Mallory and Irvine were there.

The night was one of cruel anxiety not only for Odell but also for Hazard, Norton, Noel and the others below. None of them got much sleep, wondering what had happened to their two companions. They went over theory after theory. Perhaps they had made Camp Six but had been too exhausted to come down any further. Perhaps one of them was seriously hurt in the camp and the other could not leave him. Perhaps they had been forced to spend the night in the open but had found some kind of a shelter from the bitter wind. But whatever theories they evolved to comfort themselves, the conclusion was all but unavoidable that Mallory and Irvine had died or been killed, and Everest had claimed the lives of two more of those who sought to overcome her.

After an almost sleepless night, during which gusts of icy wind, howling over the rocks and ridges of Everest, almost carried his tent off the mountain to the glacier thousands of feet below, Odell set out for Camp Six.

The porters were unable to accompany him. They were exhausted and suffering badly from the altitude —one reason being that they invariably slept with their tent so tightly sealed that they could get little oxygen to breathe in the already rarefied atmosphere. Odell sent them back down to Camp Four and after watching them to see that they came to no grief, commenced a lonely climb to Camp Six.

The wind was worse than it had been on the previous day. He had to bend double to make any progress against it. He put on one of the spare oxygen sets in the hope that this would help, but found he got little aid from it. He increased the amount of oxygen he was breathing, but the effect was only slight. He experimented by switching the oxygen off. According to the best medical opinion he should shortly experience a feeling of collapse. But when this did not happen, he decided to go on without the oxygen tube in his mouth. He was breathing hard—gasping would be a better word—but still able to climb.

Foot by foot he staggered upwards, now gaining a few yards, now bending double to rest and force more air into his lungs, now compelled to shelter for a while behind a crag or ledge from the wind which cut like a lancet through his clothing.

At last he reached the single tent which formed Camp Six at a height of twenty-seven thousand feet. With fumbling hands made stiff and painfully slow by the cold, and his heart beating like a trip hammer, he pulled aside the fly.

The tent was empty. Everything was as he had himself left it two days before. The compass he had brought up for Mallory lay in the spot he had put it. The food was untouched. The sleeping bags had not been used. Mallory and Irvine had never returned to Camp Six on that fatal day, June 8, when they set off for the summit of Everest.

Odell decided that he would climb further along the route which Mallory and Irvine had taken towards the

summit. He was not trying to reach the top of the
mountain, only hoping to find what had happened to
his two companions. He dumped the oxygen apparatus
and set out. No sun shone upon the grim citadel of
Everest. The whole bleak peak lay dark under a fore-
boding covering of clouds. The wind howled and
piped around. The snow danced and writhed about his
legs, like phantom arms plucking at him. There was
no living thing so high in the world as he, and no
place more friendless.

On he struggled. Half an hour. Two hours. Every
five minutes he had to stop and rest. The whole force
of the will had to be summoned to make every step.
Up and up he climbed alone into greater loneliness,
with the wind jibing and shrieking at him, and the
mountain crags standing around like so many tomb-
stones, full of warning.

There was no trace of Mallory and Irvine to be seen,
and no possibility of Odell getting to that rock step
near which he had last seen the two figures of the
climbers. After two hours climbing and searching in
the gale, Odell reached the end of his endurance and
was forced to turn and come down again. In his hunt
for his friends, he had climbed higher on Mount
Everest than any of the mountaineers of the expedition
of 1922 had been able to achieve. He made no mark
of the height he reached for he was not after records.
But he could not have been far short of twenty-eight
thousand feet when he was forced to turn back
brokenhearted and without news.

Back at Camp Six he was so tired that he could do
nothing but crawl into the tent and rest for a while.
Then, when there was a lull in the wind, he pulled out
two sleeping bags, and stumbling and falling, dragged
them to a snow slope and laid them out to form a letter
T, the signal for "No Trace." Flying snow prevented

him from seeing the answering signal, but one was not needed. There was nothing further he could do. The only course of action open was to return to Camp Four on the North Col.

He picked up the compass he had left confident that Mallory would return and find it, and the oxygen-breathing set. Then he closed the flap of the tent leaving inside all the other supplies. The little tent and its stores would form a monument for Mallory and Irvine as long as it stood.

Before starting his long journey down to the North Col, Odell looked back once more to the summit of Everest. He wondered whether man had dared too much in presuming to try to climb to the summit of the Goddess Mountain of the World. Perhaps this was one place in the world forbidden to man, and the mountain would kill all who trespassed in that sanctuary.

The peak took on, for a second, an almost irresistible allure. The pyramid of rock appeared out of the swirling snow and seemed to beckon him upwards. Majestic, serene, the highest point in all the world, it seemed in that instant to be the very threshold of heaven. Perhaps Mallory and Irvine, nearer the summit than he, had found themselves drawn relentlessly on, unable to turn back. Maybe they had, in fact, climbed Everest and found Eternity waiting for them at the top.

As swiftly as it had revealed itself to him, the summit disappeared again behind a veil of freezing mist. Odell turned his back on it, and weary and half blinded by the snow, commenced his descent to the North Col. Time after time, he had to shelter from the gale, to stop for breath, to peer, benumbed, through the driving snow to find his way. But at last he reached the col in safety, and with Hazard, descended the ice cliff to Camp Three. There they found Hingston and Shebbeare. After a meal, the four went down to Camp Two, spent the night and then joined the main party at the base camp. It was the end of the 1924 expedition.

New records for climbing had been set, but Everest was still unconquered. And the Goddess Mother of the World had killed twelve of the men who had pitted themselves against her.

CHAPTER THIRTEEN
Trial by Blizzard

NINE YEARS PASSED BEFORE ANOTHER EX-pedition could be sent against Everest. During that time constant applications were made to the Dalai Lama on behalf of the Royal Geographical Society and the Alpine Club for permission to attempt once more to reach the summit of the mountain.

But to each application the Dalai Lama politely replied no. The failure of the expeditions of 1922 and 1924 had undoubtedly confirmed the Tibetans in their belief that the Goddess Mother of the World was sacred. It would have been defying popular feeling too blatantly for the Dalai Lama to have allowed more climbers to try to reach the summit of the mountain so soon after seven porters had been killed in 1922 and two porters and Mallory and Irvine in 1924.

At last, in August 1932, word was relayed through the Political Agent in Sikkim and the Government of

India that the Dalai Lama had given his consent to another expedition being sent to Everest. In the interim many young men in Britain and other parts of the world had been preparing themselves for the day when another attempt on Everest would be allowed. When the news that the long sought permission had been granted was published, the organizers were flooded with letters from men of all occupations asking to join. Some were climbers experienced on the famous peaks of the world who had to be turned down because their age was against them. Others were schoolboys who had done a little rock climbing on their vacations or perhaps scaled a mountain or two. It was very difficult to say no to these eager youngsters, knowing how bitterly disappointed they would be.

After so long an interval hardly any of the old Everest climbers were available. General Bruce could not be had, nor Norton, now holding an important position in the British Army. Geoffrey Bruce was also on army duty and could not be spared. Somervell had given up his medical practice in England to work as a medical missionary in India. Eight years of India's climate had taken such a toll upon his health that he was not up to the venture.

The Everest Committee picked Hugh Ruttledge, who had spent five years in the Himalaya area and climbed a great deal with Gurkhas and Sherpas, to head the expedition, and left it to him to select his men. He asked Odell to join but the man who had made that magnificent lone search for Mallory and Irvine could not get away. C. G. Crawford, a veteran of the 1924 effort, was available, however, and willing to join in the new attempt.

Ruttledge then turned to men who had been climbing in the Himalayas recently and who would therefore be acclimatized and accustomed to the kind of

conditions to be met on Everest. One party had recently scaled Kamet, a Himalayan peak and the
highest mountain climbed up to that time. Of these he
was able to enlist F. S. Smythe, the leader of the
Kamet climb, a mountaineer of wide experience; Eric
Shipton, who though only twenty-five had made some
remarkable ascents; Dr. Raymond Greene, medical
officer; and Captain E. St. John Birnie of Sam
Browne's Cavalry, who had won himself a good name
on Kamet.

Others picked were Wyn Harris, who had made two
ascents of Mount Kenya in Africa with Shipton; L. R.
Wager, back from an expedition to Greenland; J. L.
Longland, one of the best rock climbers in England at
the time; and Major Hugh Boustead, on duty in the
Anglo-Egyptian Sudan.

Major Boustead was so determined to be a member
of an Everest expedition that he had spent all the
time he could climbing and skiing in the Alps to train
himself for the part. When he felt he had enough
experience, he had gone into the Himalayas on his
own, with a party of Sherpas, to do some climbing
there. George Wood-Johnson had also been fired with
the ambition to belong to an Everest expedition. After
talking with Shebbeare, transport officer of the expedition of 1924, he had gone to work on a tea planta-
tion in Darjeeling to learn Nepali to help to qualify
himself and also do some climbing in the Sikkim
Himalaya. T. A. Brocklebank, another chosen, was,
at twenty-four, the youngest member of the party and
had done a great deal of guideless climbing. Dr.
W. McLean, with much Alpine experience was made
second medical officer, and E. O. Shebbeare joined as
transport officer.

It was planned to be at the foot of Everest by April
of 1933, and again an enormous amount of prepara-

tion had to be undertaken in a comparatively short while. This time the plans were more elaborate than those of 1924. Special tents were designed which would stand up to the fierce gales of the mountain. Previous climbers had suffered from frostbite on the soles of their feet. One reason was that the nails in the soles of their boots conducted the intense cold through the leather. Boots were therefore made with double soles with no nails penetrating the inner sole. A wide selection of foods containing the greatest nourishment was packaged. Indeed, so complete were the preparations that they included a silk hat which was to be given to the Sherpa porter who carried his load the farthest up the mountain.

Radio receivers and transmitters were taken so that the climbers could communicate with each other and receive all-important weather reports from Darjeeling. The monsoon, coming in from the west, reaches Darjeeling a few days before Everest and so the party would be warned when to expect it. Portable telephones were another addition to the equipment. But the expedition turned down the offer of an enormous kite capable of carrying a man, and displaying the sign "Buy New Zealand Butter." Even if any use could be found for it, the kite was not likely to survive long in the one hundred mile an hour gales of Everest.

Once more oxygen was to be taken, though the dispute as to whether it was worthwhile or not still raged. Norton and Somervell in 1924 had climbed to twenty-eight thousand feet without it. So had Odell. Mallory and Irvine were the only two who had used oxygen in an attempt to reach the summit, and they had not lived to report on its value. But progress in the design of oxygen cylinders had been made in the intervening years. The weight was cut to a little less than twelve pounds, as against twenty pounds previously, and that in itself was a powerful argument for giving oxygen another try.

The journey into Tibet was completed without incident and in good weather, and the expedition arrived at the Rongbuk monastery on the glacier on April 17, 1933. A blessing was sought of the aging Lama of the monastery for both porters and climbers, and after it was given, the series of three camps up the East Rongbuk Glacier were established.

The work was done deliberately at a leisurely pace. Ruttledge had decided that he would give everybody in the party time to acclimatize so they would be in good shape for the crucial test of the asault on the summit. This year the porters seemed to have caught especially well the spirit of mountaineering as distinct from a mere job of carrying loads for white sahibs. Some were men who had carried on previous expeditions. They were proud of their ability and promised that they would "go high" on the mountain with their loads. This was a very different spirit from that which Norton had to contend with in 1924. Then he had been compelled to argue for four hours in the freezing cold to get porters to push on from Camp Five to Camp Six. Now all said with simple confidence that they would carry above twenty-seven thousand feet, where it was intended to place the jump-off camp.

But first, once again, the North Col had to be climbed.

This year the col presented a particularly vicious problem. Great domes of avalanche snow and boulders of ice lay at the base of the gleaming frozen wall. One third of the way up the col was a huge horizontal split. This would protect climbers from avalanches, but in itself was a formidable barrier to cross. Above it was a wall of blue and green ice, forty feet high at its lowest point. This wall was straight up and down. At the bottom lay a pile of avalanche snow, which could be climbed to help scale the ice wall. But that put the climbers in the path of an avalanche chute down which tons of ice and snow might come spilling at any moment.

So formidable an obstacle was the North Col that it was decided to establish a further camp, Three-A, at the foot, in which those moving up to the top of the col or descending to the glacier could rest.

It took eight days to cut steps across a thousand feet of ice and snow at the bottom of the col to reach its face. Work could be done for only a few hours each morning. Then a gale would come up out of nowhere and the men would be forced to return to their tents, the snow, swept off the ground, swirling around them waist high. This meant that each morning the steps made on the previous day had to be cleared out again.

The crevasse across the North Col was negotiated without too much difficulty and then came the job of scaling the vertical wall of ice. It was in fact worse than vertical, for the lower part overhung slightly so that a man standing face to it was compelled to lean backwards out over the glacier. Shipton and Smythe undertook the work of putting a ladder up this wall of ice. Shipton supported Smythe against the wall with the head of his ice axe while the latter drove a piton or peg into the ice as high up as he could reach. Then he cut foot and hand holds in the ice to climb up to the peg. With one foot on the peg and another in one of the holes or niches in the ice face, he hoped to be able to cut more "steps" above. But his foot slipped off the peg and he only just managed to save himself pitching over backwards to the glacier. He had to hold on to the cliff with one hand and swing his ice axe with the other to cut steps—a difficult feat in ordinary circumstances, but particularly exhausting at a height of twenty-two thousand feet.

At last, however, the rope ladder was suspended from a peg driven near the top of the overhanging section. From there on the ice sloped back, and steps could be cut to the ledge forming the top of the wall. Here Camp Four was established, actually about two hundred feet from the real top of the North Col. To put it on the top would be to expose it to the frightful gales raging across the ice cliff.

Then followed a full week of gales during which nothing could be done. It was May 22 before a start was made placing the camps on the actual sides of Everest, and by then there was a great need for speed. Radio messages told of an early monsoon setting in. Perhaps only a week of "good" weather remained before the mountain would be blanketed with snow and climbing made impossible.

Camp Five was pitched at twenty-five thousand seven hundred feet, with enough provisions for climbers to stay a night and go on the next day to establish Camp Six. Eight porters had been specially selected for this work and all were in excellent spirits. Then the weather changed for the worse once more. The wind sprang up, bringing heavy snow with it. No start up the mountain could be made. Eventually, the weather became so bad that all had to descend to Camp Four on the North Col. All the porters but one were suffering from frostbite. Greene had strained his heart in the effort to establish Camp Five.

Things got so bad that Camp Four had to be moved. It was, as already related, situated on a ledge about two hundred feet below the top of the North Col. Avalanches were constantly dropping around it. Many of the stores were buried under the snow and at any time the tents with the men inside them might be buried also. The camp was moved to the top of the col. Here the biting wind had to be endured, but at least there was no danger of those in the tents being buried under an avalanche. It is difficult to conceive of the fury of the wind. Roaring across the ice cliff, it sounded like a number of locomotives speeding through a gorge.

Now there was little to do but wait for a break in the weather. It came on May 28, when Harris, Wager, Birnie and Longland re-established Camp Five. They had with them eight porters, who spent the night at the camp. On the following day they were to carry loads of about ten pounds each up to Camp Six, which it was hoped could be placed at twenty-seven thousand five hundred feet.

This was the crucial test. If the porters could not or would not make the climb with their loads, then it would be quite impossible to get to the summit. And the higher the porters would carry their loads, the greater the chance of Everest being conquered.

The porters responded to the challenge with the greatest courage, and they well earned their proud title of "Tigers." Their names were Angtharkay, Da Tsering, Nima Dorje, Ang Tsering, Kipa Lama, Passang, Tsering Tarke and Rinzing. The first five were Sherpas, the last three Bhutias. Sherpas, as already explained, are members of a mountain tribe whose homeland is in Nepal. Bhutias are also mountain tribesmen, but are natives of Tibet. Actually they are kin one to another.

The party was ready to start at five in the morning but the frost was so sharp that even a minute in the open brought the risk of frostbite. So the departure was delayed until eight o'clock, by which time the sun had risen high enough to warm the air though not the iron-hard ground. Even then almost all suffered mild frostbite during the first few hours. Birnie, who had strained a leg muscle previously, was left at Camp Five. At a rate of four hundred feet of height an hour (though the ground covered to achieve this was, of course, much greater) all plodded steadily forward. They had much trouble from the icy slabs on the mountainside, which were treacherous, but at last reached an altitude of about twenty-seven thousand feet. Indeed, so good was the spirit of the men that they were prepared to carry their loads even further to a snow patch at the foot of the rock step below where Mallory and Irvine had last been seen.

This, however, would have taken another two hours. It was already one-thirty in the afternoon, and to make camp where they were would leave little enough time for the porters to return to the North Col before dark. Longland was to shepherd them down while Harris and Wager were to stay at Camp Six to make their attempt on the summit.

It was, however, by no means an easy matter to find a site on which the single tent, measuring no more than seven feet long and four feet wide, could be pitched. There was not a spot to be found which was level. All around were a series of stone slabs overlapping like tiles or shingles on a roof. None of these, however, was wide enough to put the tent on. At last the likeliest slab was selected, and by adding to it a platform of small stones, something approaching a level place was made. As soon as the tent was up, the supply of food and four sleeping bags and cooking utensils unloaded, the porters set off with Longland for the North Col. Wager and Harris crawled into the tent to get what rest they could and await the morrow.

Longland wisely decided to take his men down the mountain along the northeast ridge so there was no chance of losing his way on the snow and ice wastes of the north face of Everest. The sky was clear, no wind blowing and no trouble anticipated from the weather as he started. But he had hardly reached the ridge with his men, when, with a scream of fury which drowned out all other sound, the wind smote them. One minute Longland was able to see several hundred yards. The next, his vision was limited to a few feet in front of him. Their goggles became filmed with ice and had to be taken off, and then their eyelashes froze together. The snow flung itself upon the men parallel with the ground. All had to lean into the gale to remain on their feet.

The porters could barely see each other and nobody but Longland was sure of what direction they were heading. He kept them moving, for to stand still in this blizzard for even a few minutes might mean death. Some terrible doubts, however, began to play in his mind as they staggered downwards. They came across the remnants of Mallory's Camp Six, of the fatal expedition of 1924, and found lying in the streamers of torn canvas an electric torch. This still worked. But Longland recalled seeing a photograph of this particular camp, and in an agonizing moment he remembered that it was pitched not near the true ridge which led to the North Col and safety, but on another farther to the east. He might, he realized, be leading his men straight to a precipice over which they would drop thousands of feet to death on the East Rongbuk Glacier.

To hesitate, however, even to change the route, would have been to demoralize the eight men whose lives were in his hands. Longland decided to stick to his guns and follow the ridge he was on rather than cast around in the blizzard looking for another route. Faces were now caked with ice which hung in icicles from eyebrows, noses, and chins. The men's breath condensed and froze on their lips and cheeks in a rim of frost. Some of the porters began to succumb to exhaustion and sat down. Longland dragged them to their feet, and forced them to continue walking.

He kept an anxious watch all the time for a particular snow gully. If this showed up on his left, he would know that he was headed for the precipice. He would have to turn around, and whether he could get the men to follow him up the mountain slope again in search of the right way was doubtful. Very likely they would elect, in their dejection, to sit down and die where they were.

But luck was with him. In a lull in the swirling snow he at last spotted a green tent. It was Camp Five. They were safe.

While Longland was leading the men down, Smythe and Shipton had joined Birnie at Camp Five. The three kept leaving the tents to peer into the blizzard and see if there were any sign of Longland and his men. Suddenly they saw several shapes like ghosts approaching through the blizzard. Ice and snow were thick upon every part of them. They seemed like strange creatures of the blizzard, crouching as they came down the mountain. The three rushed out to find Longland leading his men safely in.

Longland's feat of bringing his eight porters down Everest in the blizzard was one of the greatest pieces of mountaineering ever performed. But all Longland had to say about it was that he was so busy keeping the men moving that he hadn't time to think of his own condition. It was only later, when he had reached the North Col, that he realized that he was close to exhaustion. He had reached Camp Five in the nick of time. A little longer and Everest would have claimed nine more victims.

CHAPTER FOURTEEN
The Vital Step

MEANWHILE HARRIS AND WAGER, AFTER A
poor night in Camp Six, were up at 4:30 on the morning of May 30 to make their attack upon the peak of
Everest. A poor night is perhaps too mild a way of ex-
pressing it. Their tent was pitched upon a steep slope
which it was not possible to level. Wager slept in the
lower part of the tent with Harris above. But Harris
kept sliding down on his companion during the night
and between the cold, the sharp stones beneath their
sleeping bags and the constant struggle to keep apart,
the two got hardly any rest. When they woke in the
morning, it was to find that the hot soup which they
had put in a thermos flask for breakfast was frozen.
No thermos flask seemed able to function in the frigid
heights of Everest.

An hour was spent thawing out boots over a cooker
which burned solid methylated fuel, and after a
meager meal and a stiff struggle to get into their
windproof clothing the two were ready to start. The
sun was hidden behind another peak and they set
out in deep blue shadows with a ten-mile-an-hour
wind blowing. So intense was the dry cold that within
minutes they were chilled to the bone. They went on
for an hour, panting heavily in the thin air. It is difficult to describe the struggle to breathe while climbing
on the upper parts of Everest. All the muscles of the

chest and stomach have to be used to heave enough
of the thin dry air into the lungs to sustain life. Every
few steps the climber has to stop, and elbows on his
knees, spend several agonizing seconds sucking in air
and expelling it in heavy gasps. This excessive panting
caused in Wager and Harris and others too a loss of
body heat and added considerably to the possibility
of frostbite.

At last the sun rose high enough to send a golden
flood of light over the upper slopes of Everest, dispers-
ing the deathly cold shadows around. Wager took advantage of the warmth of the sun to remove his boots
and massage his feet. He had been out but an hour
and already was feeling the first symptoms of frostbite
despite his specially designed footwear.

The two intended to explore the way to the top of
the mountain which had become known as "Mallory's
route" since that was the direction taken by Mallory
and Irvine when they died. In essence, this consisted
of following the northeast ridge of Everest—a sharp
profile of the mountain which rose up to the base of
the final pyramid leading to the summit. Two obstacles
bar this route—the two rock steps already referred to.
These are a few hundred feet apart, the first being
about fifty feet high and the second about ninety.
Wager and Harris climbed towards the northeast
ridge, and when they were about sixty feet below it,
found lying on the ground an ice axe. The polished
steel head was stamped with the name of the maker,
Willisch of Tasch. It must, they decided, belong to
either Mallory or Irvine, for no other climbers had
been on this part of the mountain.

Much speculation has arisen over the finding of
this axe. Some hold that Mallory reached the summit
and put the axe there as a sign that he had conquered
Everest but that it was blown to the place where it

was found by the winds. That, however, is unlikely,
as the wind would have blown the axe from the summit over the other side of the mountain. Others say
that the axe was put down deliberately by one of the
climbers because he was tired. That, mountaineers
point out, is about as likely as a seaman throwing
away a lifebelt because it is too much trouble to
carry it around. An ice axe is the saving of a mountaineer on many occasions and no one as experienced as
Mallory would part with his.

The most logical solution is that the axe marked the
scene of a fatal accident involving Mallory and Irvine.
It is possible that they were roped together and that
one of them slipped. His companion might then have
dropped his axe and tried to grab the rope with both
hands. Perhaps this is what happened, but the second
man was pulled off his feet by the first and both fell to
death on the glacier thousands of feet below. But all
this is guesswork. It is not likely that Everest will ever
release the secret of how Mallory and Irvine met their
end.

Wager and Harris left the axe where they found it
and went on to the first step. This they found to be, in
reality, two large towers. Both were too sheer to be
climbed without a great deal of time being spent on
the task. Beyond, the ridge was broken by great clefts
in the rock, some of them fifteen and twenty feet deep.
The two decided that instead of continuing along the
ridge, or "Mallory's route," they would climb along
the face of the mountain until they came under the
second rock step. Then they would be able to decide
whether to go up to the ridge from there. But when
they got below the second step, it was to discover
that there was no way to gain the ridge from where
they were. The ascent was far too steep and offered no

footholds. The only hope of reaching the summit was
to keep angling along the face of the mountain, climbing a little as they went until they got below the
pyramid which forms the peak of Everest. Then, with
luck, they might be able to struggle to the top.

The route they took was that taken by Norton in
1924. It was not exceptionally difficult. Indeed, at
lower altitudes it would be quite easy. A series of narrow ledges sloping outward and downward gave them
foothold and all went well for a hundred and fifty
yards. Then they had to round a buttress of the mountain beyond which was a deep and almost vertical
gully, fifty feet wide and heavy with powdery snow.
The angle in the gully was so steep that snow could
just rest on it. It flaked off and fell softly away at a
touch.

The gully plunged down ten thousand feet without
a break. One slip here would mean certain death for
both men, since they were roped together. They had
to be roped to give each other what support they
could, though mostly it was just moral support. They
went cautiously into the gully never looking down,
inching their way across, sweeping the snow to un-
cover little knobs of rock on which they could put
their feet. After what seemed an eternity they got to
the other side. Here another buttress, pushing out
from the face of the mountain, had to be climbed
around. The rocks sloped wickedly downwards and
had more snow upon them. With nerves taut they
eased themselves around this obstacle and went on
for another one hundred and fifty feet, climbing fifty
feet in the meantime to the edge of another and
smaller gully.

Harris tried to cross this. Clinging like a fly to the
side of the mountain, he reached out with a foot

towards a little rock ledge. He could not quite step on
to it. Perhaps with a little jump or an extra long reach
he could do it. But if he missed?

If he missed he would plunge to certain death, for
Wager had nothing to which to make the rope fast.
The peak was no more than nine hundred feet above.
If this one gully could be crossed, they could make it.

Suddenly Harris realized that he couldn't make the
crucial step to the tiny knob of rock. He was trembling
violently and his breath was coming very hard. His
vision was poor and he could not trust the coordination of his muscles. He shook his head and the two
turned around in silence. Everest had beaten them
with an obstacle which would provide no trouble at
all—if it were say fifteen thousand feet lower. They
had reached the same altitude as Norton, twenty-eight
thousand one hundred feet, and about the same place.
But there they had to give up.

On the way back they picked up Mallory's ice axe,
as it became known, and Harris left his in its place.
Wager, determined to see if the second step could be
climbed or not, got enough energy to drag himself up
to the northeast ridge. He found that the ridge consisted of a saw edge of rocks, too difficult for an exhausted man to climb over. He couldn't get any higher.
But he guessed that the same condition would prevail
up to the second step. This would make Mallory's
route impracticable. From the ridge, Wager was able
to look over the southeast side of Everest—the only
man to do so up to that time. He saw a stern ice-
clad cliff slipping steeply down, so sheer as to be impossible to climb.

The two went back to Camp Six to which Smythe
and Shipton had advanced for their turn at the mountain and told them their story. Both decided they
would take a look at the second step themselves to

make quite sure that it was impossible to climb along the northeast ridge. If this proved to be the case, they would try angling along the face as Norton and Harris and Wager had done.

When Harris and Wager returned to the North Col on the following day, both were suffering from dilated hearts. They had only one misadventure on their way down. At one point Harris decided that he would glissade or slide on his feet down a slope. But the slope had a twist to the east, leading him towards a precipice with a drop of several thousand feet to the East Rongbuk Glacier.

Quickly he turned around and threw himself down on the snow on his face. He grasped his ice axe at the ends and turned it so the pick plowed into the snow. He had to do this slowly and firmly lest the ice axe be jerked from his hand. With every second he was getting nearer and nearer to the precipice. But at last his pace slackened and he stopped, only a few feet from the precipice. Badly shaken, he rejoined Wager. There was no more sliding on Everest for the rest of the expedition.

CHAPTER FIFTEEN
Lone Assault

SMYTHE AND SHIPTON WERE FORCED TO spend a day and two uncomfortable nights at Camp Six before the weather would clear sufficiently for them to make their effort to climb to the peak of Everest. As

was the case with Harris and Wager, their attempt was
to be without oxygen. There was a repetition of the
same kind of blizzard which had caught Longland
and the porters in their descent, and the nights,
though not quite sleepless, were certainly far from
restful. Smythe reported that the sharpest stones in
Asia must certainly have been collected under the
ground sheet of the tent, so that lying down was
agony, and sitting no great improvement.

The morning after their second cheerless night
dawned clear, and both agreed they must start right
away or give up their attempt altogether. They went
through the formality of trying to heat soup for breakfast (at the altitude of Camp Six, boiling liquids can
be gulped down without pain because the boiling
point is so low) and struggled into their windproof
clothing. Smythe wore three pairs of pants, a vest, a
thick woolen shirt, and six pullovers under a suit of
closely woven cloth. Looking as much like a bull as a
man, he still was not warm. Shipton was suffering from
stomach trouble, but was determined to do his best,
and so the two set out.

Slowly the pair struggled up to the northeast ridge
of Everest and went round the base of the first step
rather than climb it. There, Shipton was brought to a
halt by spasms of pain in his stomach. He could go no
further. It had been agreed that no man climbing
Everest was to go on until he collapsed, because in
doing so he would risk not only his own life, but
that of his companion in trying to bring him off the
mountain. Smythe satisfied himself that Shipton was
capable of getting back to the shelter of the tent and
then continued alone.

It was a courageous decision to make. There was
now no one to help him in difficult places. There was
no one with whom to discuss climbing problems, and

no relief for him from the frightful depressing loneliness of the mountain wastes, remote from all living
things. But his heart was set upon making the peak if
he could, and this outweighed the hazards ahead.

He made good progress, going at an angle across
the face of the mountain as Harris and Wager had
done. In places he found the snow hard and could cut
steps in it to help in climbing. Elsewhere there were
ledges of rock, narrow to be sure, but enough to give
foothold for his spiked climbing boots. He went along
these ledges and came at last to the buttress leading
into the big gully or couloir which had to be crossed.

Only the merest knobs of rock offered a foothold
for rounding the buttress. He had to lean his body
against the face of the mountain, with his outstretched
hands groping for any fingerhold which could be
found. Thousands of feet below, in the deep shadows,
lay the Rongbuk Glacier, with nothing to break his
fall should he slip. One heavy breath, it seemed to
him, would be sufficient to send him toppling backwards to death.

Fearful of an accident, Smythe edged back to
where a ledge offered more foothold, but he had no
sooner done so than he scolded himself for letting his
nerves get the better of him. He had got through
tight places like that before, he told himself, and
there was no reason why he shouldn't do so now.
But when he got out again on the buttress, his fingers
holding onto mere pebbles for support, the weight of
his body resting on little knobs of rock, he realized
once again that he could not make it. A movement
of just a few inches away from the buttress face
would send him hurtling to his death.

Back he went again, and, descending a few feet,
found a ledge which led around the buttress into the
gully. Once in the gully he was delighted to find the

snow in it hard—so hard he could cut steps in it with his ice axe. This made it easier to get to the other side. Here there was another buttress. His plan was to go around this, climbing at an angle to a ridge at the top into a smaller gully. This last gully seemed to provide a comparatively easy route to the base of the summit.

But now he faced additional dangers and difficulties. The snow on the buttress was sheltered from the prevailing west wind, and was as soft as flour. Smythe could not take one step with the certainty that his feet would find something solid to rest upon. At times he sank up to his thighs and even his waist in this soft snow which might slip away at any moment, carrying him with it. Often he had to burrow with his hands to find a hold.

Once a knob of rock on which he was standing gave way. Only the fact that he had a second before driven his ice axe into the mountain wall above him saved him from instant death. As it was he was left dangling ten thousand feet above the glacier until he could find another rock to put his foot on and take his weight off the ice axe.

In one hour of lonely nerve-racking work he had climbed only fifty feet. It was already 11 A.M. Hours more would be needed to get to the summit at this rate. There was the possibility that at any moment one of Everest's blizzards would break on him, blowing him off the mountain like a fly off a wall. Smythe realized bitterly as had Norton, Wager and Harris before him, that there was not enough time left in the day to get to the top of the mountain, and get down again.

He looked up at the summit—no more than nine hundred feet above him. Silent and merciless, it

seemed to mock at his puny efforts to reach it. He
turned back defeated.

During his solitary ordeal, Smythe had two strange
experiences. First, it seemed to him that he was not
alone at all, but accompanied by another person who
was an experienced climber. The impression of being
with someone else was so strong that he felt they
were roped together and that if he, Smythe, fell, his
mysterious companion would save him. Once, taking
a piece of cake out of his pocket to eat, he broke
it in half and turned round to offer a piece to his
"friend." It was a shock to find nobody there.

Smythe had no explanation to offer for this strange
feeling, beyond the suggestion that odd things happened to men under conditions of great physical and
mental stress and that the effect of oxygen shortage on
the brain is not fully understood.

The second occurrence was the appearance of two
peculiar objects in the sky during his descent to Camp
Six. Smythe happened to look towards the north ridge
and saw what looked like two kite-balloons floating in
the sky some distance below him. One had squat
wings on it; the other a kind of beak rather like the
spout of a kettle. They were not moving forwards or
backwards, but seemed to pulsate slowly. He noticed
that the pulsation did not correspond with his own
breathing.

Thinking that perhaps the shortage of oxygen had
affected his eyes, Smythe looked carefully away for
some time and then glanced back again. The two objects were still where he had first seen them floating
in the air above the ridge. Then a mist started to drift
between him and them and when it went away, they
had gone.

Smythe speculated that the two objects might have

been the result of some trick of the light or mist, or
perhaps even a mirage. But he was quite sure that
he had seen them. Today they would perhaps be described as flying saucers.

When he got back to Camp Six—a difficult job because mists were now drifting over the mountain—he
found Shipton sufficiently recovered to go down.
Smythe himself, however, was so tired that he decided to spend another night in Camp Six while Shipton went on to Camp Five.

But Everest had not finished with them yet. Shipton had been but an hour on his way down to Camp
Five when without the slightest warning, a blizzard,
similar to the one which had struck Longland, struck
him. Weakened by stomach trouble as he was, unable
to see more than a few feet ahead, incapable of climbing back to the camp above or descending to the one
below, all Shipton could do was crouch behind a rock
until the first fury had spent itself.

The blizzard let up for a few minutes and Shipton
made a number of spurts down the mountain, shelter-
ing where he could when the necessity arose. But as
he groped through the blinding snow that swirled
around him, he completely lost his sense of direction.
He could tell only which way was down, but whether
he was headed to the safety of the North Col or a
precipice he did not know. At one point, he had to
lower himself from a rock to a bank of snow below.
But as soon as his feet were upon it, the snow slipped
away, leaving him dangling in the air. His hands,
numbed by the cold, commenced to slip off the rock.
But by a tremendous effort he managed to drag himself up again.

At last he saw the North Peak ahead during a lull
and reached Camp Five. There Birnie made him as
comfortable as he could with hot tea and something

to eat. Birnie himself was suffering from frostbite and undernourishment, but was as cheerful as a boy on a holiday. However, there was but one small tent, and one sleeping bag. Another tent was available but would have to be erected. In the howling wind, their hands numbed beyond feeling, neither man could get the second tent up. They slept together in the same sleeping bag and the next day got down to Camp Four.

Smythe meanwhile spent a good night at Camp Six. When the blizzard struck he was worried about Shipton, but could do nothing for him. He was glad, however, that he had not continued to try to reach the summit for he would have been caught by the blizzard and killed.

The next day he got breakfast with the last of the fuel in the tent and started out for the lower camps. And once again the blizzard struck. Three nights and two days at altitudes of twenty-seven thousand four hundred feet and over had left him with no reserves of physical strength. A frightful cold seized his limbs, penetrating with a deadly grip through muscle and bone. This was the final danger signal before perishing from exposure. He knew that if he could not find some place in which to shelter from the wind, he must die.

He struggled on. At times he was reduced to crawling on hands and knees. The wind made a plaything of him, knocking him down, sending him slipping down the mountain with only his ice axe to stop himself. His goggles were iced up. When it seemed that all hope of survival was gone, he came across a ledge sheltered from a wind—a small haven of peace in the fury of the storm. It was so quiet here that he could even feel the warmth of the sun through the ragged grey clouds overhead. A few feet above him the fury of the wind sounded like peals of thunder.

Then the sun completely disappeared and, fearing that the blizzard would increase in wrath, Smythe decided to chance getting down to Camp Five. He made fair progress and when he was only three hundred feet from the camp was heartened to see two men emerge from it. They were Shipton and Birnie. He shouted and started tottering towards them. But they neither saw nor heard him. They turned and went down the mountain leaving him to stagger with his remaining strength to the camp.

When he got there, it was to face another blow. Shipton and Birnie had collapsed the tent to save it being ripped away from its moorings. The only thing to do was to go on to Camp Four.

At this point his legs were so weak they would hardly support him. They gave way under him without warning. He staggered from side to side, stumbled, recovered, fell, got up again, and forced himself to keep going. When it seemed he could go no more, Longland, down on the North Col, spotted him. Longland was suffering from frostbite and had been warned not to expose himself to the cold. But he came a thousand feet of the way towards Smythe, who could now progress only by inches. Eventually the two reached each other and Longland gave Smythe a thermos bottle of hot tea laced with rum. This revived him sufficiently to reach the safety of the camp.

Strangely enough, when Smythe was subsequently examined by McLean, the expedition's chief medical officer, he was found to be one of the few men who had climbed high on Everest and had not suffered from a dilated heart. Yet as a boy he had had a weak heart and had been discharged from the Royal Air Force at twenty-seven as unfit.

Despite the failures of Wager and Harris and Smythe and Shipton to reach the summit, it was decided that a third attempt would be made, this time with oxygen. But the weather forbade the project. The snow piled deeper and deeper on the mountain. The North Col, heavily covered, threatened avalanches and all plans for a third attempt had to be called off.

Everest was still supreme.

CHAPTER SIXTEEN
Another Victim

BY THE MID-1930S EVEREST WAS EXERTING a world-wide fascination. A host of suggestions as to how the mountain might be climbed flooded the Mount Everest Committee in London. They came from those with experience in mountain climbing and those with no experience at all. One man had a theory of his own and determined that he would put it to the test.

He was Maurice Wilson, an Englishman, thirty-seven years of age in 1934. He believed that by abstaining from food for a short period and by living a very rigorous life, the powers of the human mind and body could be enormously increased. So strongly did this belief possess him that Wilson was bent upon drawing world attention to it. The best way to achieve this end, he decided, would be to climb Mount Everest alone!

His original plan was to crash-land an airplane near the summit of the mountain, climb to the top and then come down. He went to India, bought a plane and learned to fly. But news of his plan reached the authorities and they impounded his plane.

Wilson, deprived of his airplane, decided to climb all the way up Everest from the bottom. He hired a few of the Sherpas who had accompanied the expedition of 1933 and, disguised as a Tibetan, slipped into Tibet and made his way to the Rongbuk Valley. The journey was in itself a tremendous feat for an inexperienced and poorly equipped traveler. He introduced himself to the Lama at the Rongbuk monastery who had proved such a friend to members of the previous expeditions. The Lama was greatly impressed with his sincerity and wished him well.

Wilson went off without his porters up the East Rongbuk Glacier, quite certain that he would soon reach the top of Everest. He had a small tent and a modest supply of rice. He struggled up to nineteen thousand five hundred feet—again an enormous achievement for an unexperienced man—and was driven back by blizzards. He was compelled to rest for two weeks. Then he started out again, this time taking the Sherpa porters with him.

Just beyond Camp Three of the expedition of 1933, he found a food dump, whose supplies were very welcome. His Sherpas here refused to go any further. It was apparent to them that Wilson was no mountaineer, and they were not prepared to risk their lives with an unskilled leader. So they left him. Wilson, however, went on and reached the North Col. He had probably anticipated finding the steps still cut up the face of this huge cliff of snow and ice from the expedition of the previous year. But they had all disappeared.

Time and again with enormous determination, Wilson tried to get to the top of the col only to have to turn back. Then there came a day when he could not leave his tent. He stayed inside growing weaker and weaker until at last he died. His body together with his diary in which the last entry was dated May 31, 1934, was found by a reconnaissance expedition in the following year. The tent had been torn to shreds by the wind. Only the guy ropes still remained anchored in places.

Mount Everest's toll of her would-be climbers was now thirteen.

In London application was once again made by the Everest Committee for permission to send another expedition to the mountain. This time the Dalai Lama agreed to an attempt or attempts being made from June 1935 to June 1936. Unfortunately this would be too late in 1935 to take advantage of the pre-monsoon weather. So a climbing attempt was out of the question for that year.

However, it was decided to send a scouting force which would serve a number of purposes. All efforts to climb the mountain had been made before the monsoon broke. But the question had been raised whether it would be possible to make an attempt during the monsoon or immediately afterwards. Again, the various expeditions had always tried to climb the mountain along its northeast ridge going up the East Rongbuk Glacier. Mallory, it will be remembered, had scouted the possibility of climbing from the west but had decided the job would be too great from that direction. Still, there just might be a way which Mallory had missed in which the mountain could be tackled from the western ridge. The scouting expedition of 1935 was charged with the job of settling these questions one way or another. The expedition also provided an opportunity to test mountaineers who could take part in the climbing attempt set for the spring of the following year.

It was a small party that left Darjeeling for Everest in May of 1935. Eric Shipton was in charge and he had with him five experienced climbers: H. W. Tilman, Dr. Charles Warren, Edwin G. H. Kempson, E. H. L. Wigram, and L. V. Bryant, the latter a New Zealander. Michael Spender came as surveyor to make a record of the surroundings of the mountain. Only fifteen Sherpas were engaged and expenses were kept as low as possible. Lavish, generously equipped expeditions apparently did not have more chance of winning through to the summit of Everest than smaller ones. The problem was more to have the right kind of weather than an enormous quantity of supplies.

At Rongbuk all were well received by the Lama, who praised the spirit and character of Maurice Wilson. Then the party went up the East Rongbuk Glacier to test the snow on the North Col as a first task. They found the frozen body of Wilson together with his diary near the old Camp Three. He was buried in a crevasse in the glacier.

The mountaineers, having arrived at the North Col, set about testing the condition of the snow. It answered very well to all the tests, seeming to be firm and good for climbing. They went on up the col and Shipton and Kempson established a camp on the top without difficulty. The only trouble came from the Sherpas, who after the finding of Wilson's body refused to go on. They said Wilson's death was a bad omen. But a man-to-man talk put the heart back into them again, and they laid aside their fears.

Shipton proposed to erect another tent at twenty-six thousand feet on the mountain and examine the condition of the snow up to and around twenty-seven thousand feet. Food for fifteen days was brought up to the North Col camp, and the examination of the snow was to be done by Shipton, Warren, and Kempson with the aid of nine Sherpas.

The snow on Everest, as pointed out earlier, does not behave like that on any of the great mountains in Europe. When it should be packed solid it is often light and powdery. When it appears solid on the top, it is frequently loose and dangerous below. Thus, this study of snow conditions might prove immensely valuable for later climbers.

So far the weather had been excellent—little or no wind and warm bright days, for the monsoon period is a comparatively warm season in the Himalayas though it brings heavy snowfalls. The whole mountain was covered at this time. Once the camp had been established on the North Col, the weather broke. Snow fell heavily for four days without any sign of a letup. A sortie was made up the mountain, but the climbers had to turn back after going only a little way because of the weather.

Fearing that they all might be weakened by continuing to live in the exposed North Col site, Shipton decided to descend to Camp Three on the glacier. And then a grave discovery was made. The climbers had gone down the face of the col only two hundred feet when they found that hundreds of tons of snow had avalanched below, the debris being spread over a wide area on the glacier. This was bad enough, but what was more disturbing was that no one had heard the avalanche, and the snow which had peeled off the slopes was the same which they had tested for three days in climbing the North Col and had seemed perfectly safe.

In view of this avalanche of "safe" snow, it was imperative to get off the North Col right away. Shipton gambled that his party would be safe in descending immediately since it was unusual for one avalanche to follow another. If they waited, however, there would be a risk of another avalanche occurring. Down they went then, without mishap, to reach Camp Three in safety.

The party now split up to go about its various tasks. Some idea of their activity can be gained from the fact that in two months they climbed twenty-six mountains, with Tilman and Wigram ascending seventeen of them. Much of this was pure sport. But experience was gained and one fact was definitely established. The snow on the Himalaya mountains about twenty-three thousand feet never packs hard or freezes during the monsoon season. Thus, it would be useless to try to reach the summit of Mount Everest during the monsoon. Snow conditions alone would defeat the climbers.

However, there was still the task of exploring the west side of the mountain. Wigram and Tilman climbed to a col on the foot of the west ridge and found the lower part of the ridge quite unscalable. This dashed any hopes of tackling Everest from that side. Shipton and Bryant, however, went up the West Rongbuk Glacier where they could peer behind Everest to the south side. They saw the great ice fall which Mallory had noted. It was like a monstrous series of rapids which had been frozen solid. This ice fall descended into a glacier called the Khombu. Above the ice fall it was suspected was another col, given the name of the South Col. But neither Shipton nor Bryant got a glimpse of this. The presence of the South Col was deduced only from their experience of mountain formations. Their conclusions, therefore, were mixed. They could not rule out an attack upon Everest from the south until they knew more about

it. But they could not find out more about it until
permission to explore was obtained from the government of Nepal. The southern side of Mount Everest
lies in Nepal, a land as jealous of its territory as is
Tibet.

Its work done, the reconnaissance party of 1935 returned to England. They had established that Everest
could not be climbed during the monsoon, and that
it could not be climbed from the west. Whether it
could be climbed from the south was in doubt.

Meanwhile in London preparations had been made
to send a climbing expedition to Mount Everest the
following spring. Ruttledge, who had led the expedition of 1933, was again put in charge and he chose
eight climbers for the effort. They were Smythe, Shipton, Harris, Kempson, Warren, and Wigram (all of
whom had been on Everest before) and two new
men for Everest, P. R. Oliver and J. M. L. Gavin.
Oliver had done some climbing in the Himalayas six
years previously, so only Gavin was without experience on the world's highest mountain range. However, he had plenty of Alpine climbing behind him.
C. J. Morris was selected as transportation officer, W.
R. Smyth-Windham was to be in charge of radio com-
munications and Dr. G. Noel Humphreys was taken as
medical officer.

The party arrived at Rongbuk on April 26, 1936.
There was little or no snow on the slopes of the mountain and the weather was good. But a plume of snow
a mile long, streaming off the summit of Everest, gave
a grim warning of the fury of the wind which would
have to be battled at the peak.

This expedition was equipped, as had been that of
1933, with a radio transmitter and receiver. The most
modern type of oxygen equipment was also taken.
Five days after arrival, when the lower camps on the

East Rongbuk Glacier had been set up, a radio warning was received of bad weather setting in. The same
afternoon the skies over Everest became suddenly
clouded and snow started falling. Soon the whole
mountain was covered with snow. This was a bad sign
indeed, for normally heavy snow is not expected on
Mount Everest until June.

Still the work of stocking the camps up to the North
Col continued and in the middle of May Camp Four
on top of the col had been set up and was occupied by
Smythe and Shipton, who had forty-two porters with
them. The porters were in fine spirits, quite confident
that they would be able to carry loads as high as
twenty-seven thousand eight hundred feet, where the
jump-off camp was to be placed.

However, Everest was now heavily blanketed with
snow. It was so thick on the north ridge, which had to
be climbed in the initial ascent of the mountain, that
it was quite hopeless to try to get through it. After
waiting for three days for an improvement in the
weather, which did not come, Camp Four was evacu-
ated the following day and the whole party withdrew
to Camp One. There it would be easier to keep in good
physical condition until the weather improved.

But the weather did not improve. Instead a radio
message on May 19, the day Smythe quit Camp Four,
told of the arrival of the monsoon at Ceylon, the island
off the southern tip of India. On May 23, only four
days later, the first monsoon snows fell upon Everest.
The monsoon had swept across India in the astound-
ingly short period of four days.

Nonetheless, the climbers went up the glacier again
to Camp Three in the hope that this was not the true
monsoon, but only a forerunner of it. They believed
they might yet have a fighting chance to make an attempt at climbing the mountain. But the North Col,

thick with snow, was too dangerous to climb, and they returned again to Camp One. Once more they advanced when the weather improved a little. It was decided that the climbers, working in pairs under the supervision of Smythe, would make their way in relays up the North Col. Harris and Kempson would make a route up the first five hundred feet to be succeeded by Warren and Wigram and so on.

The snow looked as though it were ready to avalanche at any moment. Indeed, the debris of a small avalanche was found at the base of the col. The first five hundred feet were successfully climbed. But beyond that, conditions were too dangerous to be risked. The snow gave every indication of being ready to slide. Even if the climbers could make the top, it was doubtful that the porters could follow them. Shipton, who had seen in the scouting expedition of 1935 how the North Col snow could avalanche unexpectedly, canceled the venture. Reluctantly, all returned to the glacier.

The next morning a heavy northwest wind raged over Everest. When it subsided a little, Shipton and Wyn Harris got permission to scout the col and see if they could find a safe way to the top for the porters. To their delight, they found the snow now firm. Steps could be made in it with a hard kick. The two climbed about five hundred feet without trouble, and came to a place where it was necessary to climb at an angle instead of directly up. Here they roped together. Shipton went ahead, Harris remaining where he was, paying out the rope which linked them.

All went well for ten or twelve yards. Suddenly there was a sharp crunching noise. The whole slope of snow on which the two men were standing commenced to slide down towards a four-hundred foot drop off a precipice of ice. Shipton was knocked down

and fell on his back. Harris leapt off the moving snow
to the lip of a horizontal crevasse, drove his ice axe
into the snow and managed to loop the rope around it.
It was the same tactic which Mallory had used to save
his three companions many years before. The rope
jerked tight as it took the strain, but the ice axe,
although Harris leaned all his weight on it, began to
pull out. The avalanching snow piling around Shipton, who had been checked by the rope, was more
than Harris could hold.

Then, when it seemed either that Harris must let
go or follow Shipton to death over the ice cliff, the
avalanche stopped. Shipton was only a few feet from
the edge of the precipice. He picked himself up carefully and the two men went down to the bottom of
the col.

After that all attempts to climb the mountain that
year were called off. The expedition of 1936, despite
heroic efforts, was beaten by the weather before it
could get well started.

CHAPTER SEVENTEEN
Snowed Out

DESPITE ALL THE REBUFFS, THERE WAS NO
thought of giving up the efforts to reach the summit of
Everest. If anything, determination hardened, and
each expedition which returned unsuccessful represented a challenge to send another and yet another.

The defeats of the past were not a dead loss by any

means. A great deal of knowledge about Everest and the conditions which would be met in climbing the mountain was gained. It was known, for instance, that men could climb to within a thousand feet of the summit without using oxygen. Many held that it would be possible to reach the summit without oxygen. Indeed, there was (and is) a hard corps of climbers who look upon the use of oxygen as unsporting—rather the same kind of thing as a yachtsman turning on an auxiliary engine during a sailing race. They feel that man, unaided by stimulants, should get to the top of the mountain.

Again, it was established that the Sherpa porters could carry their loads above twenty-seven thousand feet. And a corps of porters whose whole heart was in the task had been developed through the years. They differed greatly from those who in 1922 could see no point in trying to climb the mountain and carried only for the pay. Now the pay was secondary to a large extent. The honor of being on an Everest expedition mattered more to the Sherpas. Those who by carrying their loads above twenty-six thousand feet earned for themselves the title of "Tiger" were immensely proud of their achievement.

It had been found also that all climbers must thoroughly acclimatize themselves to altitude, and take things as easy as possible before the actual assault. The mountaineers learned to keep in condition but not overtax their strength. Finally, one mountaineer, Harold W. Tilman, showed that a small expedition might have as much chance to reach the top of Everest as a large and expensive one. Many others shared his view.

Tilman, who had taken part in the reconnaissance expedition of 1935, had failed to qualify for the 1936 attempt because it was thought that he could not acclimatize himself to the higher altitudes. But while the 1936 attempt was being made, he and N. E. Odell climbed Nanda Devi in the Himalayas, a twenty-five thousand six hundred and forty-five foot peak and the highest mountain to be scaled at that time. The party which conquered Nanda Devi was a small one, with supplies kept to essentials.

When, therefore, permission was received to send another climbing party to Mount Everest in 1938, Tilman was asked to lead it. He introduced some radical changes. A man with definite views on diet, he decided to provide only the plainest of food, eliminating many of the luxuries which had been taken on previous expeditions. He wished only a small party and took but six men besides himself. They were F. S. Smythe, N. E. Odell, E. E. Shipton, C. B. M. Warren, Peter Lloyd, and Captain P. R. Oliver. The only newcomer was Lloyd, who had a wide experience of Alpine climbing.

Tilman, hoping to profit from the fate which had overtaken the expedition of 1936, decided to get to the Rongbuk Valley at the earliest possible moment. He actually arrived there on April 7, which was ten days earlier than any expedition had reached the valley. In the interests of economy and mobility, he brought no radio apparatus, holding that while radio could inform him of the weather, it could do nothing about it. When he arrived, the weather was clear, and Everest devoid of snow. The camps along the glacier were set up and stocked by April 26, but by now most of the climbers were suffering from colds or sore throats. A fierce wind was blowing which could be felt keenly in the glacier camps. It would be several times more severe up on the exposed North Col.

So it was decided that rather than expose the whole party to frostbite by tackling the North Col, they should go down to the Kharta Valley to recuperate. This was the valley which General Howard-Bury had scouted out in the reconnaissance expedition of 1921, a fertile, warm haven to the east of Everest.

They remained there for several days, but on returning to the Rongbuk Valley on May 14 were horrified to find the mountain completely blanketed with snow. Two weeks earlier Everest had been snow free, yet the weather too cold to be endured. Now the weather was warmer, but the mountain so heavy with snow there was little prospect of being able to ascend it. It looked as though the weather had already defeated the 1938 expedition as it had defeated the previous expedition in 1936.

Nonetheless, Tilman was determined to see what could be done. The North Col was finally climbed in the face of heavy snowfalls and Camp Four set up and occupied. Tilman, Warren, and Odell, in spite of the snow, made an effort to climb up the north ridge. They got only as high as twenty-four thousand five hundred feet and then had to give up. Tensing Bhutia, a Sherpa porter who had first served with the Everest expedition of 1936, was with them, and acquitted himself well, helping to break a trail up the slope for some part of the way.

This first attempt to climb on the mountain served one useful purpose. Two types of oxygen apparatus had been brought along. One was the "open" type weighing twenty-five pounds, by which air and oxygen could be breathed at the same time. The other, the "closed" type weighing thirty-five pounds had a face mask and the wearer could breathe only oxygen from his cylinders. Warren tried this latter type and found that far from doing him any good, he couldn't breathe at all, and came near suffocating.

The evening of their first effort more snow fell.

There could be no doubt now that the monsoon had
already started, and this despite the fact that Tilman
had got his expedition to the foot of Everest earlier
than any previous climbing party. It was just bad luck
that the monsoon was also early, bringing with it
warm day temperatures to make the snow slopes unsafe, and clouds of soft flaky snow which covered the
mountain deeper and deeper. The party retreated to
the base camp with the faint hope that the weather
might improve.

Then, without the slightest warning, the weather
changed for the better. A wind came up from the west
blowing the snow in clouds off the upper part of
Everest. The sky was clouded over with a dull grey
veil, meaning that day temperatures would be low,
making what snow remained safer for climbing. Tilman decided to climb the North Col again, but this
time from the west side. It was felt that this side was
less likely to avalanche. The climb was made without
mishap, although the remains of an enormous avalanche which had fallen only a few days earlier were
lying at the base of the ice cliff.

Fifteen porters and four climbers, Tilman, Smythe,
Shipton, and Lloyd, then were on top of the col at
Camp Four on June 5 and set off the following
day to place further camps up the side of Everest,
hurrying to make the best use of the change in the
weather.

The snow on the lower slopes of the mountain,
which they had waded through hip deep only a few
days before, was now crisp and firm. The party went
up without trouble to twenty-five thousand feet, but
here the effect of altitude began to tell on the porters.
Two of them could go no further and had to be left
with their loads to rest. The Sherpa, Tensing Bhutia,
however, plowed along like a Trojan. Three hundred

feet short of the site for Camp Five one of Everest's
unpredictable snowstorms struck. Smythe and Lloyd
were ahead with Shipton and Tilman bringing up the
porters. The porters said they would go no further.
In the raging storm they had to be cajoled into struggling along, and at last got to the site for Camp Five
at twenty-five thousand eight hundred feet.

Here it was found that one of the loads which had
been left behind with the porters who could come no
further was a tent. That meant that Smythe and Lloyd
and seven porters who were to remain at Camp Five
would have to share a tent meant to acommodate no
more than four. But Tensing Bhutia and another
Sherpa named Passang volunteered to go down and
get the other tent, which they did.

Tilman and Lloyd now returned to the North Col
with six porters, leaving seven with Shipton and
Smythe. These would carry the stores for Camp Six,
the jump-off camp, and then return, leaving the two
climbers in a position to make their attempt to reach
the summit.

The next day the wind blew hard from the east.
It was not unwelcome, for Shipton hoped that it
would blow some of the snow which had fallen the
previous day off the upper part of the mountain. He
and Smythe delayed their departure for a day, and
then in better weather were able to establish Camp
Six, at twenty-seven thousand two hundred feet. The
porters did remarkably well, but hopes that the snow
would have been cleared away by the wind, or at least
frozen to provide a firm footing, were not realized.
Powdery and treacherous, the snow blanketed the
upper part of Everest, so that each step had to be
made with care lest an avalanche be started or a
climber lose his footing and fall to his death.

The porters got safely down the same day, leaving

Shipton and Smythe in a position to make an attack on the peak, which was eighteen hundred feet above them. They ate supper—a little cocoa and glucose. Neither had an appetite nor was able to sleep much. Shipton had brought a book with him, but oxygen shortage so affected him that he found it impossible to concentrate on his reading. He found that he could not understand much of what he read even when exerting all his mental powers.

At 3:15 the following morning they started their climb for the summit. It was hopeless to try to cross at an angle to the big gully where others had blazed a trail previously. The way was deep in snow and dangerous in the extreme. Their only hope was to climb directly to the northeast ridge and see whether a way could be found to the peak from there. Climbing was heartbreaking work. So early in the morning, the cold was intense. It seemed to stab the throat and lungs with each breath. Hands and feet were numb in a matter of minutes and both men were in grave danger of frostbite. In the end, they had to return to the tent and wait for the sun to rise. When they started out again, it was to find themselves wading through snow up to their hips. An hour's hard work took them only forty feet, and this was on the easier slopes. The more difficult part lay ahead. They persevered until they got to a place where they met downward sloping slabs of rock, covered with a foot or more of snow. Here progress was utterly impossible. Even to try to climb was to invite death from falling. Both men were in good shape. In better weather they would have had, they believed, a good chance of reaching the summit. However, as conditions were, there was no chance of getting near it. They had to turn back.

Tilman and Lloyd tried next but met with no better luck. They were brought up against a rock face which could not be climbed. There was no way round it. One side was a steep cliff and on the other they sank to their waists in snow. They also had to turn back.

That was the end of the expedition of 1938. On the way down to the North Col, Lloyd, mistaking the route, fell into a crevasse. He was not roped to Tilman, but luckily the crevasse was not very deep and so he was pulled out, though he spent some cold and lonely minutes in an icy prison waiting for help to arrive. When the two climbers got to Camp Four on the North Col, it was to find one of the porters, Passang, sick and lying alone in a tent. His right side was para- lyzed. He could not talk, eat, or dress himself. The other porters shunned him, holding that his condition was a judgment of the gods. Everest, they said, de- manded a victim and it would not be wise of them to help Passang. The best thing to do was to leave Passang as a sacrifice to the gods. Tilman was sur- prised that even those porters who had seemed to be the sick man's special friends were unwilling to make any move to help him.

Tilman made it clear that there were going to be no victims offered to the gods of the mountain, and no paralyzed men left to die on its sides. Eventually, the porters got the point that Passang was to be taken down. They did not go at the task with any relish, but the paralyzed porter was eventually carried down the North Col and treated by the expedition's doctor. What caused his paralysis is still in some doubt. But the suggestion was made that it resulted from a blood clot forming in the brain as a result of his exertions at high altitudes. He had carried a load, as had some of the other porters, up to Camp Six, and with Tens- ing, had gone back to pick up the tent which the other porters had been unable to carry further.

So ended the expedition of 1938, defeated by Everest's weather as so many attempts before had been.

Then the world was plunged into World War II and plans to conquer the mountain were put aside, though not forgotten, for twelve troubled years.

CHAPTER EIGHTEEN

Attack from Nepal

THE END OF WORLD WAR II BROUGHT, AS one of its indirect results, the closing of the Tibetan gateway to Mount Everest. In the years before World War I, the threat of Russian penetration led to the opening of Tibet to Britain. But after World War II, the Chinese Communists took over Tibet. That meant that for an indefinite period no British climbers could hope to tackle Mount Everest from the Rongbuk Glacier. Yet just as one door to Everest closed, another opened.

The government of Nepal in previous years had been unwilling to allow mountaineers from other nations into its territory. But starting in 1947, the Nepalese authorities relaxed their attitude. Several expeditions were allowed to climb in the Nepal Himalayas. The change in attitude on the part of Nepal raised the question of whether Everest could be climbed from the southern or Nepalese side. One American party, led by Dr. Charles Houston and including his father and Harold W. Tilman, was permitted to approach the Nepal side of Everest. But time was short and little exploring of the upper approaches to the mountain from Nepal could be done.

There were, however, a great number of arguments against such an attempt—arguments advanced by mountaineers with plenty of experience of Everest. Mallory, for instance, had climbed a pass which looked down on the south side of Everest during the reconnaissance of 1921. A scene of wild and forbidding confusion confronted him. There was a steep drop of fifteen hundred feet from the pass to a glacier below. This glacier was the Khombu. It flowed out of a rift between the sides of two mountains—Everest and another mountain called Nuptse, or West Peak. In its flow through this rift the glacier tumbled a great distance (two thousand feet it was later discovered) so that the ice of which it was composed was smashed into mammoth blocks and ridges, many as high as houses. Such a condition on a glacier is called an ice fall. It is much the same thing in a glacier as rapids are in a river, though the waves of the rapids are replaced by towers and blocks of ice, separated by massive crevasses. Enormous labor would be needed to climb up this ice fall. What lay beyond?

Mallory was not able to see past the ice fall for the Khombu Glacier bends to the north and his view of its upper reaches was obstructed. He did, however, see that above the icefall the glacier occupied a huge basin which he called the West Cwm. (Cwm is a Welsh word, pronounced koom, and it has the same meaning as the English word "combe" or bay.) Mallory suspected that at the head of the huge basin was another col connecting Everest with an adjoining peak, Lhotse, or South Peak.

The existence of this new col, called the South Col, was partially confirmed during the reconnaissance of

1935. But no one had had a plain view of it. Mountaineers hoped that this col, like the North Col on the other side, would provide a stepping-stone to Everest. But it was likely to be very much higher than the North Col. The question was, could it be reached? Could a party, with porters, get up the frightful ice fall on the Khombu Glacier? If they did, could they get to this South Col? And if they succeeded in reaching the South Col, would they be able to climb to the top and so get to the slopes of Everest from the southern side?

Some of the older mountaineers believed that any such attempt must fail. The North Col, they pointed out, had provided a tough enough obstacle with its one thousand foot sides of ice and snow. This South Col, held to be much higher, would be more than could be climbed.

Then there was the matter of getting stores up the ice fall and up the col. Finally, these same stores would have to be carried up the slopes of Everest by exhausted men to place camps up the mountain side. No, the critics said. An attempt on Everest from the southern side in Nepal was out of the question.

But others were not so sure. One enthusiast, Michael Ward, proposed to the Himalayan Committee of the Royal Geographical Society and to the Alpine Club that the Nepalese authorities be asked to allow a British reconnaissance expedition to explore the South Col and the Nepal side of Everest. The upshot of it all was that the required permission was given and Eric Shipton, who returned just at the right moment from China, was put in charge of the party.

It consisted, beside Shipton, of W. H. Murray and Michael Ward, who had been prime movers in promoting the reconnaissance, and Thomas Bourdillon. Another mountaineer, Campbell Secord, who had helped get the reconnaissance approved, was unable to come. Later two other climbers from a New Zealand Himalayan expedition, E. P. Hillary and H. E. Riddiford, joined Shipton and his companions. These together with Dr. Dutt, an officer from the Geological Survey of India, completed the party. All were on their way by the middle of August, 1951.

The route to the mountain led through Sola Khombu, the homeland of the Sherpas. Shipton was particularly anxious to visit the place which bred these fine mountain men. Shortly after he arrived in India he was met by one Sherpa, Angtharkay, who had been with him on some of his previous expeditions to Everest and other climbing ventures. He was, in fact, an old friend, and took care of the porter problem. There were some troubles and adventures in crossing India to Nepal, and getting to Sola, but all were overcome. One mishap, however, was particularly strange. In climbing a steep cliff, the porters unwittingly disturbed a hornet's nest. In a second they were attacked and stung unmercifully by the angry insects. Two were so badly stung that they developed a high fever. All had grotesquely swollen faces. But they recovered the next day.

When Shipton and his men got to the country of the Sherpas, they found a welcoming party waiting for them in each village. They were taken to the porters' houses and so much hospitality lavished on them that it looked as though they might not get to the Khombu Glacier. At last, however, base camp was established on the glacier at the foot of a mountain called Pumori, which is twenty-three thousand one hundred and ninety feet high. The party was now surrounded by mountains, all of them giants, and these formed, as it were, the outer defences of the great fortress of Everest.

Everest and its southern surroundings can best be pictured by thinking of a football stadium many miles long. The football field is represented by the Khombu Glacier. But it is not level or smooth. It rises through a height of several thousand feet from one end to the other, and its surface consists of a riven, torn, wilderness of ice. Across the middle is an ice fall where blocks of ice as big as houses and weighing thirty and forty tons and more are jammed and toppled and thrown upon each other.

Through this, the mountaineers and their porters would have to climb, reduced by the chunks of ice around to the size of ants. Beyond, at the upper end of the field, past this appalling line, is the upper basin or West Cwm. The sides of this monster stadium are composed of some of the world's tallest mountains and the ridges or cols between them. On the south or right hand side is first of all Nuptse, or West Peak, soaring twenty-five thousand six hundred and eighty feet into the skies. At the far end, and still on the right, is Lhotse, or the South Peak, twenty-seven thousand eight hundred and ninety feet high. The connecting ridge between them forms the right hand side of the stadium. On the left hand side is Everest itself, its huge western ridge forming the left side of the stadium. At the far end is the col between Lhotse and Everest, the South Col. It was this col which had to be climbed to get upon the slopes of Everest. It is twenty-five thousand eight hundred and fifty feet high— nearly three thousand feet higher than the North Col on the other side of the mountain.

But when Shipton and his men arrived, none had yet seen the South Col from the Khombu Glacier. All hopes of being able to climb Mount Everest now depended on two things. First, would it be possible to find a way up through the ice fall—a way safe enough for laden porters to pass along? Great quantities of stores must be brought through this tumbled wilderness of ice for the camps which would have to be placed up the sides of Everest with the last one as near to the top as possible. Second, would it be possible to climb the South Col?

To settle these two questions was the main objective of the expedition, and the members went about the problems as soon as they had established their base camp on the glacier at the foot of Mount Pumori.

On September 30, Riddiford, Ward, Bourdillon and two Sherpas, Passang and Nima, went off to explore the ice fall. Passang was not the same man who was paralyzed on the North Col in 1938. The name Passang (or Pasang) is quite common among the Sherpa people. Meanwhile Shipton, Murray, and Hillary decided to climb one of the many buttresses of Pumori. By getting up high they would be able to see up the ice fall into the West Cwm and get a bird's eye view of the difficulties. They hoped also to get the first view ever had of the South Col from this side.

Luck was with them. Hillary and Shipton climbed to just over twenty thousand feet and were able to see through their binoculars the whole terrain laid out before them in crystal light. In the far distance lay the West Cwm and beyond it the glittering sweep of the South Col. The upper end of the cwm was about two thousand feet higher than they had anticipated. They could see, however, that it should not be difficult, given good snow conditions, to get onto the South Col. But it would be best to reach the South Col by climbing the sides of Lhotse and then striking out at an angle for the col. The walls of the col themselves looked too steep to be climbed.

Now they turned their attention to the ice fall, which was the first obstacle to be dealt with. It was not a

straight fall, but twisted in a left-hand spiral. The monster blocks of ice were forced first one way and then
another in a corkscrew pattern. Up the center, and at
an angle across the fall, lay a possible corridor. But
the fall was a good two thousand feet in height.
Niagara Falls, for comparison, is only one hundred
and sixty-seven feet high on the American side. Yet
the comparison must not be taken too far, for the ice
fall of Everest is not a direct drop. The view obtained
by Hillary and Shipton was very encouraging. But they
had one reservation as they descended from their
perch on Mount Pumori. The central corridor through
the ice fall provided an excellent chute for ice avalanches to hurtle down. And these avalanches were to
be expected. The mountain cliffs on the left-hand side
of the fall were festooned with hanging glaciers.
Hanging glaciers are something like icicles as big as
city blocks. Pieces weighing many tons break off
them constantly in the warm weather, smashing down
with a roar like thunder.

Meanwhile, Riddiford and Passang had explored
one section of the ice fall at close quarters and had
made such excellent progress that they had been able
to advance a considerable distance up it. The others of
the ice fall party, Ward, Bourdillon, and Nima, had
tried another route, but found their way led through
such a forest of ice pinnacles that they could not get
to the ice fall proper.

Nonetheless, the progress made was most encouraging. It seemed as if the ice fall might be passed
through, and beyond Hillary and Shipton had seen a
way to get to the South Col.

But the task was not to be so easy. On October 2,
Riddiford, Hillary, Bourdillon and Shipton with three
Sherpas, Passang, Dannu and Utsering, took a tent to
the foot of the ice fall intending to try to climb it the

next day. But that day it snowed, not hard but persistently and since the weather was comparatively warm, the snow remained soft upon the ice and unsafe for climbing. The party had to wait out the day.

There was one remarkable occurrence. In midmorning, a roaring sound was heard and taken for the noise of an ice avalanche falling down one of the adjoining peaks. However, it continued minute after minute until it seemed that all the mountains around must certainly be ridding themselves of their festoons of ice in an unprecedented cataclysm of avalanches. Yet nothing was to be seen, though the party waited fearfully. The roaring continued and finally it was discovered that the noise was caused by the wind tearing across the tops of the mountains which towered around. It was a grim warning of the kind of wind the climbers would have to battle on the heights of Everest.

The next day was fine, although soft snow coated the entire area. Because of the mountain walls, the whole glacier was in deep shadow and would remain so until late in the morning. Nonetheless, the men set out, though they had to stop frequently to take off their boots and rub some warmth back into their feet. They waded most of the time up to their knees in snow, but progress was good. The tracks made by Riddiford in his previous exploration were still visible, and following these Shipton and the others came, after nearly four hours hard work, to the point on the ice fall where Riddiford had turned back.

Now, however, the sun had risen high enough to clear the tops of the mountains. Bitter cold was replaced by almost unbearable heat and blinding light. The sun's rays glinted off the pinnacles of ice which surrounded the explorers. Climbing in a world of tumbled ice blocks and wading to their knees in snow, they suffered from the heat so much that they had to strip down to their shirts. All perspired freely and became acutely thirsty as a result of moisture loss. The climbing itself was not very difficult, though the stillness of the hot air, the blinding white light, and the frustration of rarely being able to see more than a few feet ahead, made it slow work. Often the climbers took a likely path through the ice blocks only to find themselves up against an unsurmountable wall, or one which, though they might have scaled it themselves, would prove too difficult for porters carrying heavy loads.

At last they reached to within a hundred feet of the top of the ice fall. They were out of the gigantic ice blocks now, and before them lay a slope of snow. When they got to the crest of this, they believed they would be in the West Cwm with easy traveling ahead to the South Col.

It was the turn of Passang, the Sherpa, to take the lead. This was a dangerous place. The snow was soft, and the slope quite steep. At the bottom of the slope was a deep crevasse waiting to engulf them. The men started carefully up the snow slope. When they were but forty feet from the top, the snow commenced to avalanche.

Passang, with great skill, leapt from the sliding snow to the portion which remained stable and jammed his ice axe into it. Hillary got a firm hold with his axe on an ice block, and Shipton was able to scramble off the moving snow. But Riddiford was swept over the edge of the crevasse. There he was brought up short by the rope which linked him to the other men. For several minutes he dangled upside down in the blue-green depths of the crevasse with the snow falling all around him. Despite the strain, the others managed to hold him, and when the avalanche had disappeared into the crevasse, were able to pull him out, unhurt though shaken.

The accident might easily have been fatal to all but for the skill and quick thinking of Passang and the other two.

Now, even though only forty feet from the entrance to the West Cwm, they had to turn back. It was too late to continue and, in any case, there was little to be seen that had not already been viewed by Hillary and Shipton from their perch on Mount Pumori, some days previously. The party made their way down safely and well content. They had found a route through the ice fall, and the next task was to make it safe for porters to come up with tents so that the West Cwm and the slopes of the South Peak and the South Col could be explored.

CHAPTER NINETEEN

So Far and No Farther

TWO WEEKS PASSED BEFORE AN EFFORT was made to penetrate the ice fall again, this time with porters carrying stores. There were several reasons for the delay. First, there was a great deal of snow on the South Peak. Shipton and his companions knew from experience that this snow, being above twenty-three thousand feet, would not consolidate and was likely to avalanche. By waiting there was a chance that northwesterly winds would set in and blow most of the snow away. Also several of the party were not yet acclimatized. Two weeks of waiting would give them a chance to get fit.

During the waiting interval, the climbers divided up to explore other areas around Everest, and on October 19, Hillary and Shipton, who were working together, were back at their base camp on the Khombu Glacier. The others had not yet returned from their explorations, so these two decided to go up to the ice fall, and took with them a large double-skinned tent which would accommodate twelve men.

Two days later they had made a good route deep into the ice fall, and prepared a site for a light tent among the huge boulders of the fall to provide a half-way resting place. Then they went on to finish the rest of the route up to the West Cwm. It was a bright, windless morning and they had with them two Sherpas, Angtharkay and Utsering. All went well for some time. They followed the old route, stamping down the snow and cutting steps where needed for the porters to follow. Unexpectedly, they came to the edge of a big crevasse where the ice had split open right across the route. It took some time to find a way around this, but it was eventually bridged. But not a hundred yards further, they were surprised to find that a frightening change had taken place on the ice fall.

When first they went through it, they had been surrounded on all sides by towers and blocks of ice, as big and bigger than houses. Now these lay smashed and thrown all around as if some giant hand had knocked them down the way a child would scatter piles of toy blocks. The whole ice fall, thousands of tons of it, had moved suddenly downward during their absence, and the jar had toppled the great blocks of ice over like playthings. It was lucky they had decided to leave the fall for two weeks instead of immediately starting a route through it for the porters. Otherwise, all might easily have been killed in the "icequake."

The question was whether the ice fall would move again, and whether the surface they were now standing on was solid. The men roped together, leaving a hundred feet of rope between each man. Hillary took the lead and all commenced testing the ice with blows of their axes. It gave a booming, hollow sound. No one could decide whether the ice was hollow merely directly below or over the whole area. Then, without warning, a block of ice fell in front of Hillary, plunging through the surface of the glacier, and the whole ice fall rumbled and shook. The two Sherpas threw themselves to the ground in panic. For a minute it seemed as if the ice would collapse downwards carrying them to certain death. Then the roar subsided and the trembling stopped.

Ahead the ice was a patchwork of cracks and fissures. At any moment it might give way. It was plain that the ice fall, thawed to some extent by the monsoon weather, was breaking up and moving downwards. Even more depressing was the discovery that at this time of the year, at least, a route made through the ice fall one day might be quite unusable a day or two later. The only thing to do was to return to the camp.

Hillary and Shipton decided to let a few days pass while the other members of the party returned from their explorations.

In the meantime, they climbed some of the heights around to get a bird's eye view of the ice fall and see whether there was a safe way through the shattered area. But none could be found. Across the fall, like a swath cut through a field of corn, was a wide area of tumbled ice pinnacles and towers, though above this, all seemed stable.

When the others returned, it was decided that all would go to the ice fall to see whether conditions had changed for the better. They found they had hardly changed at all, but this was a gain on the negative side. It meant that for the time being, at least, the ice fall was not moving, and so there was some hope of going up through it. Nevertheless the porters were highly alarmed. They were not carrying loads. But they constantly pointed out that it would be extremely dangerous to carry anything up through the shambles of ice which might start sliding down at any time.

To this Shipton agreed, though all the climbers were still anxious to see whether they could reach the West Cwm. They went on, past pinnacles of ice forty and fifty feet high, so delicately balanced it seemed that one shove would topple them; and at last arrived safely at the final snow slope on which they had been avalanched during the first ascent. Here a big pillar of ice had fallen to bridge the crevasse at the foot of the slope. It provided a method of crossing to the top of the slope. Bourdillon cut steps up this ice bridge and all were able to cross over. But it was certainly no safe path for laden porters. The ice bridge might collapse without warning and send all on it hurtling into the green and blue depths of the crevasse. On top of the snow slope, the climbers found themselves in the mysterious West Cwm proper, and pressed forward, only to be barred from further progress almost immediately.

Stretching across the glacier which formed the floor of the West Cwm was a gigantic crevasse, a hundred feet or more in width. It would be the work of many days to cross this. Beyond lay others. There was nothing for it but to go back.

Two things, however, had been established for certain.

First, the slopes of the South Peak had been seen from a distance and provided a not too difficult route by which to reach the top of the South Col.

Second, the ice fall could be climbed, and would probably be in better condition in the pre-monsoon season than later in the year. With this knowledge, the expedition returned to England, eager to have one more try at climbing the Goddess Mother of the World, this time from the southern side.

CHAPTER TWENTY
The Swiss Attempt

BACK IN ENGLAND AN UNEXPECTED AND somewhat delicate hitch occurred. It was found that the Swiss had applied to the government of Nepal for permission to try to climb Everest, and this permission had been granted. Even if the Nepalese government were willing to give a permit for a British expedition to make the attempt also, nobody wanted such a thing. It would not be in the spirit of mountaineering to introduce national rivalries and have two teams racing up the mountain in competition with each other.

On the other hand the British had done all the

pioneering work on Everest. The Swiss generously offered to allow British climbers to join their expedition, making it a joint British-Swiss party. For some time this was considered. But there remained the delicate question of whether a Briton or a Swiss should lead the party. In the end it was decided not to make up a mixed expedition. If the Swiss succeeded in reaching the top of Everest, the only sporting thing to do would be congratulate them on their achievement. So close was the cooperation between the Swiss and the British climbers that the Himalaya Committee made available to the Swiss expedition all the information which had been obtained about the southern approaches to Everest during the Shipton reconnaissance.

The Swiss set off with high hopes in the spring of 1952, determined to make two attempts on Everest. The first would be launched in the spring in the lull before the monsoon set in. The second would be made in the fall when the monsoon was over and when it was believed that there would be another lull in the weather.

The Swiss expedition, organized by the Swiss Foundation for Alpine Research, was under the leadership of Dr. Wyss-Dunant. The climbers were André Roch, Raymond Lambert, René Dittert, Dr. Gabriel Chevalley, René Aubert, Léon Flory, Jean-Jacques Asper, and Ernest Hofstetter. Three scientists accompanied them: Professor A. Lombard, geologist; A. Zimmermann, botanist; and Madame Lobsiger-Dellenbach, ethnographer, one who studies racial aspects of people. They had a very compact oxygen apparatus of the "closed" type—that is, one supplying pure oxygen through a face mask. The oxygen containers weighed only two pounds.

One hundred and seventy-five porters were placed

under the leadership of Tensing Bhutia, the veteran "Tiger" who had been with the British during the attempts of 1935, 1936, and 1938. A base camp was established by April 20 on the Khombu Glacier at sixteen thousand six hundred feet.

Four of the climbers, Dittert, Aubert, Hofstetter, and Lambert with seventy-five porters went up the glacier to a height of seventeen thousand two hundred and twenty feet and put up Camp One. Next came the task of scaling the first obstacle—the huge ice fall which had to be climbed to get to the upper part of the glacier. The climbers were twice turned back in their effort to find a way through the massive boulders of ice and across the crevasses with which the ice fall abounds. Eventually another camp, Camp Two, was pitched half way up the fall.

A whole chapter might be written of the Swiss adventures in trying to get through the ice fall. The only clear route was a "corridor" to the left or north of it. But this passed directly below a series of hanging glaciers. Shipton had decided against going up this corridor because huge chunks of ice might fall at any time, killing or maiming all who were using the route. Yet no other way could be found. Roch, Flory, Asper, and Hofstetter went up this corridor trusting to luck that they would not be caught in a bombardment of ice from overhead. They got to the top of the ice fall without trouble. But there they found a big crevasse. It was sixteen feet wide and so could not be jumped. That meant they would either have to descend into it and climb out the other side, or construct some sort of a bridge across.

They came back to Camp Two and after a night of discussion set out again. Asper volunteered to be lowered on a sixty foot rope into the depths of the crevasse. Then he set himself swinging like a pendulum until he reached the opposite wall. There he was able to cut steps in the rock-hard ice up to the top. Once he was across, a bridge of ropes was passed to him, and he made it fast. Thus a way was made for the Sherpas to carry their loads over the crevasse.

Camp Three was set up on the other side of the crevasse and the work of provisioning it completed. The porters had to carry their loads up the corridor under the hanging glaciers and although several times boulders and blocks of ice fell from the west ridge of Everest into this passage, no one was hurt. But there were some near escapes. Once an ice avalanche fell into the corridor just a few minutes before a party of porters were due to pass up it.

Two more camps, Four and Five, had to be set up before an assault on the South Col could be made. The first was placed on the upper glacier or west basin at twenty-one thousand one hundred and fifty feet and the second on a glacier coming from the South Peak or Lhotse at twenty-two thousand six hundred and thirty feet. The plan was to climb at an angle on the lower slopes of the South Peak to a spur which jutted out near the South Col, called by the Swiss the Éperon des Génévois or the Geneva Spur. A dump of food was carried up to this spur and a hand rope put up between the dump and Camp Five to help in getting to it.

On May 24 it was decided to make the first attack. Lambert, Flory, Aubert, and seven Sherpas under Tensing Bhutia were to form the party. The names of the Sherpas under Bhutia were Pasant, Da Namgyal, Phu Tharkay, Ang Norbu, Mingma Dorje, and Arjiba. The first attempt was defeated by a heavy snowfall.

The following day the party started again. Arjiba had to go back because he was ill. The rest, however,

reached the dump on the spur without mishap. There
they rested for a while. Their immediate object was to
place Camp Six on the South Col. Then they were
to go on to about twenty-seven thousand five hundred
feet on the southeast ridge of Everest and put up
Camp Seven. If possible, they were to make a firm
track up the mountain to Camp Seven to help the assault party which would come after them.

But the task was beginning to prove more than they
bargained for. After climbing another thirteen hundred feet from the food dump at the Geneva Spur,
Mingma Dorje and Ang Norbu suffered the first
symptoms of frostbite and had to be sent down. This
meant the others had to divide their loads. Two thirteen pound tents were carried by Flory and Lambert,
and Aubert took a sleeping bag. But he dropped this
and it rolled down the slope never to be found again.
Its loss was a serious one as it meant that someone
was going to go without a sleeping bag on the frigid
heights of Everest.

By now the sun had set and a keen subzero wind
sprang up. The condition of the party, caught in the
open and at night, was serious. They were still below
the col and had no hope of reaching it that day.
The problem was to find some level spot where a tent
could be pitched. It was seven in the evening before
such a place was found—a hollow in the snow where
a platform for two tents could be scooped out.

All squeezed into the two tents, dressed as they
were. There was no opportunity or inclination to remove climbing boots. A few minutes in the cold out
of the shelter of the flimsy tents was more than a man
could stand. The sleeping bags could not be unrolled.
There was not room in the tiny tents for them. Tensing
managed to brew some tea which was passed around
and helped a little. The men spent the night roped

together on the wind-stricken slopes of the South Peak.
Lambert was so fearful (and with good reason) that
the wind might blow their tiny tents away, that he
drove his ice axe as an anchor into the snow and tied
to it the rope linking the men. In that way, should
the tents be blown away, the mountaineers and their
porters would still have a chance of surviving.

The night which followed was one of the most
dreadful in the history of mountaineering. There was
nothing hot to drink and no sleeping bags. The men
were so crowded together that they could not move
much and their limbs became cramped. Sleep was
out of the question and the thunder of the wind and
flapping of the tents made conversation impossible.

The next morning all were up early and struggled,
stiff and numb, up the slope of the South Peak until
at last, climbing an ice boulder at twenty-six thousand
feet, they found the South Col below them. The crest
of the col looked like the surface of a steaming white
lake. But the steam was snow and particles of ice
writhing over the frozen ground before a bitter wind.
The men climbed down to the col and pitched a tent.
The wind was so strong that they had to work on
their hands and knees. Standing for any length of time
was impossible.

This was Camp Six. The plan now was for the
Sherpas to go down and bring up more stores to be
used to provision Camp Seven higher up. Camp Seven
was to be the jump-off camp. But after their bitter
night with nothing but a little tea to sustain them,
and their weary day of carrying, the Sherpas were
exhausted and could do no more. The day was spent
in Camp Six, but that night everybody managed to
get some rest.

The following day three of the Sherpas were sick
and had to be sent back. But not Tensing. Nothing

seemed to be able to daunt the spirit of this sturdy
little climber who had pitted himself against Everest
three times before. With the three Swiss mountaineers,
Flory, Lambert and Aubert, he set off up the southeast
ridge in a heavy wind. This wind never died down
during the Swiss attempt. It remained, cruel and un-
relenting, raking the climbers with a spindrift of
snow and ice hour after hour. On they went, Tensing
and Lambert on one rope, Flory and Aubert on another. The way was not exceptionally difficult in itself
but called for heroic efforts in the below-zero cold.
By three in the afternoon the four men had attained
a height of twenty-seven thousand five hundred and
fifty feet and were on the true ridge of Everest.
Tensing had been carrying the tent all the way; he
suggested that they pitch camp here.

Flory and Aubert went back to the South Col,
leaving Tensing and Lambert to spend the night in
the tent and make an attempt on the summit the
next day. These two remaining men were in a truly
hazardous condition, for they had no stove, no sleeping bags, and nothing to drink except a little water
made by melting snow over a candle.

To keep themselves warm and prevent frostbite,
they had to spend most of the night slapping each
other. This kept their blood circulating. Rarely has
such determination to achieve a common goal been
shown by two men of such different backgrounds—
Tensing, the Sherpa from the upper valleys of Nepal,
and Lambert, a European from faraway Switzerland.

The next morning both were suffering acutely from
the effects of the severe cold. Muscles were stiff and
subject to cramps. Quite simple movements, such as
sitting down or standing up, required enormous effort. But neither would go back. They had three bottles of oxygen and some food. With these they went

on, determined to reach the summit.

Step by step they toiled slowly upwards. They found they could use the oxygen only when standing still. It was impossible to breathe through the face masks when they were moving. When they rested and took some of the oxygen, they felt revived. But the feeling left them as soon as they moved again. One second they would feel that they could make the summit. The next they doubted they could take as much as a single step forward.

Snow and mist added to their troubles. At every third step they had to halt and suck oxygen hungrily into their lungs. When they stood still, they sank to their knees in the snow. It took enormous effort to go on for three more steps. And then they had to stop again and repeat the performance.

At last, both realized they could go no further. The weather was getting worse and worse. Clouds rolled across the face of Everest. Snow commenced to fall heavily. At a height of twenty-eight thousand two hundred and fifteen feet—a bare seven hundred and eighty-seven feet from the summit and the highest yet achieved—Lambert and Tensing had to turn back.

At Camp Six on the South Col, Tensing collapsed into a coma. To keep life in him they had to forcibly awaken him time and again and force him to drink something warm. He had done more than any Sherpa before him had achieved, assuring himself a place among the immortals of Everest.

Dittert, Roch, Asper, Hofstetter, and Chevalley, who had by now come up to Camp Five, next made an attempt on the summit, setting out on May 29. Only five Sherpas were willing to go with them, and of these only two, Mingma Dorje and Sarki, agreed to continue up to the camp on the South Col. They arrived there at six in the evening after a hard day;

and that night were unable to sleep because of the wind and cold.

The wind was even worse in the morning. It was impossible to leave the camp for more than a few minutes without hands becoming so numb that an ice axe could not be held. Three of the Sherpas went down and the two who stayed, Dorje and Sarki, could go no higher. Another night had to be spent in Camp Six in the hope that the wind would die down.

The next day the wind was worse than ever. Again the day had to be spent in the camp. Sarki became gravely ill. Dittert decided that nothing more could be done. All efforts now would have to be concentrated on getting safely down with the stricken Sherpa. Then fortune favored them. They were granted a day of fine weather. It would have been an excellent day for an attack on the summit. But three nights in Camp Six had taken such a toll of the seven men that it was all they could do to get back down off the col.

As it was, they got only as far as the Geneva Spur. There Sarki was too exhausted to go further. Three of the party stayed with him while the rest descended to the lower camps by moonlight. On the following day Sarki was brought down successfully. That ended the Swiss attempt of the spring of 1952.

A second try was made by the Swiss in September of the same year. The expedition was under the command of Dr. Gabriel Chevalley and he had with him Raymond Lambert, Jean Buzio, Ernst Reiss, Gustav Gross, and Arthur Spöhel. Professor Norman G. Dyhrenfurth of the University of California joined them as photographer, and the Sherpas were under the command of Tensing Bhutia, who was making his fifth attempt on Everest.

This time the ice fall was found to be in a much better condition for climbing and a safer route was opened through it than had been used in the spring. Tree trunks were used to cross the crevasses in the fall and Camp Five was established at the foot of the Lhotse, or South Peak, Glacier without trouble.

The weather was much milder than it had been in May but the wind could be heard roaring past the high peaks on every side. Because of the warmer weather, which melted the snow deep below the surface, avalanches fell frequently from the South Peak and other mountains.

Late in October, Gross, Lambert, Tensing, and Buzio began making a route up the South Peak slopes. The lower third of these slopes was ice, and steps were cut in it and a hand rope fixed to help the porters up. On October 31 Chevalley and Spöhel went out with some Sherpas to test the oxygen apparatus. Suddenly a block of ice broke loose from a pillar on the Lhotse Glacier. It shot down a gully aimed directly at the climbers.

Two Sherpas and Spöhel were high enough up in the gully to be out of danger. Below were Chevalley and two porters and not far from them six more porters. All heard the ice block fall and crouched to the ground to try to avoid it. The ice block struck Mingma Dorje on the face and chest, killing him outright. Chevalley was knocked down but, protected by his oxygen apparatus, received only minor injuries. The others escaped with bruises. When it seemed that the danger was past, three Sherpas, tied together by a rope, fell and slid six hundred feet down a slope to the glacier below. Considering the distance of their fall, the injuries were not serious. One had a fractured collar bone and the others damaged ribs.

Mingma Dorje, whose face and chest had been

crushed by the ice block, was one of the best of the Sherpas. He was twenty-five when he was killed and he was buried close to the mountain where he died.

After this tragic accident, the work went on. Camps Six and Seven were established on the South Peak Glacier and Camp Eight finally erected on the north side of the South Col.

Then on November 20, Lambert, Reiss, and Tensing made an assault on the summit. But the mild weather of a month earlier had now been replaced by bitter cold. A forty-below wind swept Everest as the men plodded slowly upwards. Limbs became leaden. Deep cold settled into the nerves and muscles. Ice axes could hardly be held, let alone put to use. At twenty-six thousand five hundred and seventy-five feet the climbers were forced to turn back to their camp. They waited two days for the weather to improve, but the wind and cold continued. The attempt had to be abandoned.

Everest remained unconquered after ten efforts to reach her summit, and fourteen lives had been lost.

But man, though many times driven back, had not surrendered. The following year the British would try again.

CHAPTER TWENTY-ONE
Last Barrier

IN OCTOBER 1952, WHILE THE SWISS EXPEDI-tion was making its second try for the summit of Everest, the Royal Geographical Society in London announced that a British attempt would be made on the mountain in the spring. Colonel Henry C. J. Hunt, who during World War II had been Chief Instructor of the Commando Mountain and Snow Warfare School, was chosen to lead the expedition, and twelve climbers and specialists were to make up the party.

They were G. C. Band, T. D. Bourdillon, Edmund P. Hillary (the last two had been on the Shipton reconnaissance in 1951), R. C. Evans, W. G. Lowe, who like Hillary is a New Zealander, C. W. F. Noyce, Dr. L. G. C. Pugh, physiologist, A. Gregory, T. Stobart, photographer, Dr. M. P. Ward, medical officer, M. H. Westmacott, and Major C. G. Wylie, who was organization secretary. To these one further name was added: the Sherpa, Tensing Bhutia (or Bhotia Tensing Norkey as his name is sometimes given). Tensing was indeed the veteran, for he had taken part in every Himalayan expedition, British or Swiss, since 1935, and was obsessed with a determination of an almost religious quality to get to the summit of the Goddess Mother of the World.

This expedition was perhaps the best equipped and trained of any sent against Everest. Not only were all the men experienced mountaineers, but thorough tests of the equipment were made before the expedition set out for Nepal and the Khombu Glacier.

Particular attention was paid to the oxygen apparatus. Up to this time there was still considerable doubt about the value of oxygen as an aid to climbing. The Swiss had reported that it revived them at extreme heights when they were at rest. But when they set out again, Lambert and Tensing had found that weariness immediately returned.

Two types of oxygen equipment were taken. An open circuit type would allow the climber to breathe both air and oxygen at the same time. A closed circuit apparatus would give him pure oxygen only. The oxygen sets were tested in laboratories, on the Alps and on English mountains, in conditions as close as possible to those found on Everest. Further tests were given them when the expedition arrived in the mountains around Everest which form the out works of the great citadel. They stood up well in all trials.

Since it was planned to put the final camp on Everest as near as possible to the summit, selected porters were trained in the use of the oxygen equipment. It was intended that those who were called upon to carry loads high up the mountain should have oxygen to help them. This was a departure from previous practice, when oxygen had been available for the climbers only. The Sherpas were delighted with the oxygen, and made a sport of climbing with it, remarking that it made going up as easy as going down.

All then arrived in good spirits and good health on the Khombu Glacier early in April 1953 and while further training with oxygen and tests of the apparatus were being made, Hillary, Lowe, Band, and Westmacott with five Sherpas and a number of porters went off to explore the ice fall.

The ice fall was in an even more chaotic and forbidding state than it had been either during the reconnaissance expedition of 1951 or during the Swiss attempts of 1952. It was slashed throughout with crevasses, many concealed by snow. Giant pillars of ice were tossed and tumbled around in every position. Some looked as though they were ready to topple at any minute. And from all around, the sunlight, caught at a thousand angles, flung blinding, searing rays so that although they were in a freezing wilderness, the heat and light were almost insufferable.

It was the work of several days to establish a safe
route through this scintillating jumble of ice. The
problem was not merely one of finding a way through
which one or two men could pass. A route must be
discovered safe enough for trains of porters, carrying
heavy loads, to travel along. The snow had to be
packed down until it was hard, and time and again,
when this had been done, there would be a heavy
snowfall in the afternoon so that the route must be
stamped out again. The weather was good enough,
but it had settled into a routine of bright mornings
and snowy afternoons. Because of the huge mountain
walls around the ice fall and the West Cwm, the sun
does not reach them until midmorning. So work in
the early hours was bitterly cold.

Eventually three camps were established of a pro-
jected eight which were to serve as staging areas for
the attack upon the summit. Camp One was near the
base of the ice fall, Camp Two in the middle of it,
and Camp Three at the top. But the route up the ice
fall itself was a source of constant anxiety. The cataract
of ice was moving slowly all the time. Crevasses
opened up frequently, around which ways had to be
found. A well beaten path one day would be blocked
by ice chunks or cut across by deep chasms the next.

One thing worked in the party's favor. The huge
crevasse at the top of the fall which had defeated the
members of the 1951 reconnaissance had been replaced by a smaller one. That is to say it was smaller
by comparison. At its narrowest point it was about
fifteen feet across, but it was soon bridged by a sec-
tional ladder and gave no further trouble.

By the end of April the ice fall route was established
and most of the stores needed for the assault on the
summit of Everest had been brought up to the West
Cwm. And by the end of the first week in May, the

slopes of Lhotse, or the South Peak, had been climbed to a height of twenty-four thousand feet in an effort to blaze a way to the South Col.

As already stated, it is not possible to climb from the West Cwm directly to the top of the South Col. The steep sides of the ridge, blanketed with snow which may avalanche at any time, forbid this. So the mountaineers decided to climb up the less steep sides of the South Peak (Lhotse) to a height of about twenty-six thousand feet, and then, angling over to the left, reach the South Col. From the South Col they could get to the South Ridge of Everest and so climb toward the summit. The stern quality of Everest's defenses is illustrated by the fact that nowhere is it possible to climb directly onto the mountain's sides. A stepping-stone, represented by a col, must always be used.

The side of the South Peak, which had to be climbed to reach the South Col, was made up of a sheet of ice reaching from the base of the mountain to the summit. The problem then was not unlike that in the fairytale in which the hero is called upon to climb a glass mountain. This ice wall was in parts covered with snow—snow of that same loose quality which had proved so dangerous in the attempts on Everest from the north. Colonel Hunt himself led the first attempt up the "glass wall" of Lhotse and had with him Evans and Bourdillon. Later Ward and Wylie joined them and the result of their work was a satisfactory test of both types of oxygen apparatus, open circuit and closed circuit, and the discovery that a way could be made up Lhotse to the South Col.

Colonel Hunt proposed to make two and possibly three attempts upon Everest's summit. To understand the plan of attack, it is necessary to form a picture of Mount Everest from the south side. Two ridges ascend steeply to near the summit of the mountain. Where they meet they form a peak, called the south summit, which is about twenty-eight thousand five hundred feet high—five hundred feet lower than the true summit of Everest. One of these ridges, the southeast ridge, descends to the South Col. The South Col is twenty-five thousand eight hundred feet high—not very much lower than Annapurna which the French carried so magnificently in 1950.

It was planned, then, that the climb would be made up the ice face of Lhotse onto the South Col, from there up the southeast ridge to the south summit of Everest and then on to the true summit, two hundred and twenty feet above. The big mystery was what kind of difficulties would be met between the south summit and the true peak of the mountain. No one had seen the ridge connecting these two summits. The first attempt would be made directly from the South Col by two climbers, Bourdillon and Evans, using the closed circuit oxygen apparatus. This, it will be remembered, is the type from which pure oxygen is breathed. The apparatus had been tested and worked well enough. But it had some disadvantages of a technical nature and the open circuit type was more favored.

In a sense, the attempt of Bourdillon and Evans would be a dash for the peak with limited hope of success. If they got to the South Summit and could bring back information on what kind of climbing lay between this and the true summit beyond, they would have done splendidly. If they got to the true summit, they would be heroes indeed.

Should they fail, however, to reach the top of Everest, another attempt would be made the following day by Hillary and Tensing Bhutia. This would be the first time that this stout-hearted Sherpa or in-

deed any Sherpa had been appointed one of the
climbers by a British expedition. Tensing had, of
course, been one of the climbers on the Swiss party.
And he had proved himself a splendid man in every
way. All felt that it was nothing less than his due
that he should be picked over other mountaineers
from Britain for the attempt.

Hillary and Tensing, however, were not going to
try to rush the peak. They would be accompanied by
porters from the South Col who would carry a camp
for them as far up the slopes of Everest as they
could. The two would spend the night at this camp,
and, the following morning, if the weather held, make
their attempt. But before any assault could be
launched, the enormous task of erecting a series of
camps up the face of Lhotse and on the South Col
had to be completed. It was a grueling job, hard on
climbers and Sherpas alike. Bedding, fuel, food, tents,
oxygen—all had to be brought up a trail laboriously
stamped up the glassy sides of Lhotse.

The Sherpas did magnificently. On the first attempt
to reach the South Col, five out of six became too exhausted, though using oxygen, to go further. Only
Noyce and one Sherpa, Annullu, were able to reach
the col where, on the grim plateau of ice and snow,
they found the forlorn shreds of the camp erected the
previous year by the Swiss. The next day, however,
twelve porters announced themselves ready to carry
their loads to the South Col and all but one of them
made it.

A second carry was necessary. Six at once volunteered and they included one man, Dawa Thondup,
who at forty-nine was the oldest member of the
expedition. This was the first time that any porter
had carried a load twice to the South Col in the same
expedition.

At last, on May 24, all was ready. Camp Seven had been established on the South Col. Bourdillon and Evans, in good physical condition, spent the night there. On the following morning they would make their dash for the summit.

All that was needed was luck—and good weather.

CHAPTER TWENTY-TWO

The South Summit

THE ATTEMPT OF BOURDILLON AND EVANS to reach the summit, which was to have been made on May 25, was delayed for twenty-four hours.

It was delayed because both men were in need of rest after a strenuous climb up the slopes of Lhotse onto the South Col. So the whole of May 25 was spent in resting, and after a comfortable night, the two prepared to make their assault on the morning of May 26.

But immediately they ran into difficulty. The valves on Evans' oxygen set had frozen during the night and although a full hour was spent in trying to get them cleared, nothing could be done with them. Colonel Hunt, who had joined Evans and Bourdillon on May 24 as leader of their support party, therefore set off up the mountain ahead of them. His was not an effort to reach the summit but rather, with the aid of two Sherpa porters, to carry stores as far as possible up Everest to establish Camp Eight. This camp would not be used by Bourdillon and Evans, who were to try to get to the summit, if weather permitted, in one day. It was to be occupied by Hillary and Tensing when they made their attempt later. It would be their jumping-off place for the summit.

Colonel Hunt also met with difficulties. He had hoped to have two Sherpas to help him carry the stores for Camp Eight, but only one was well enough for the job when the time came. That meant that he and the remaining Sherpa, Da Namgyal, had to divide the third man's load between them. They had been underway only half an hour, however, before they were overtaken and passed by Bourdillon and Evans. The latter had finally managed to clear his oxygen valves and both were going strong.

From the South Col, the route towards the summit of Everest leads for a way through a steep gully. Bourdillon and Evans plowed steadily up this, moving well despite the fact that the snow was loose. In places where bare blue ice was revealed, steps had to be cut with ice axes. But the weather held and the two made fair progress.

Evans continued to have trouble with his oxygen set. Each stop to fix it cut their dwindling hopes of attaining the summit, besides taking a heavy toll on Evans himself. Even so the two were able to climb at a rate of nearly six hundred feet of height an hour, though the actual distance traveled was much greater than this. By one in the afternoon they had reached the top of the south summit of Everest, a height of twenty-eight thousand seven hundred feet, and five hundred and eighty-five feet higher than any men had climbed before.

Had they not been delayed by the freezing of Evans' oxygen apparatus and uncertain as to its future

behavior, they might have had a chance to reach
the true summit of Everest. But their instructions
were not to take unjustifiable risks. There was ahead
of them the problem of returning to the South Col,
and little hope of being able to do this before dark
if they tried to go on to the summit. It took perhaps
as much courage to turn back only three hundred
feet below the peak of Everest as it would have taken
to go on. But the decision was a deliberate one. They
turned their backs on a chance to be the first men to
top Everest because it was in the interests of the expedition as a whole that they do so. To have gone on
would have been not only to risk death, but also
jeopardize the chances of success of Hillary and
Tensing who were to follow.

But Evans and Bourdillon had achieved one very
important objective of their climb. From the top of
the south summit, they were able to see the true summit of Everest clearly, and the ridge which led up to
it. This ridge had not been seen before. It was hidden
from observers below by the south summit. It represented the big question mark about the final step in
the climbing of Everest. Could it be ascended? Or was
it so steep, or so heavy with snow ready to avalanche,
that it could not be climbed?

The sight that unfolded as Evans and Bourdillon
reached the top of the south summit was at once fearful and challenging. Before them was a sharp tri-
angular ridge leading up to the top of Everest. On
one side it fell away sharply in a precipice. The other
side, less steep, still slipped off at a treacherous angle.
Jagged teeth of rock thrust out along this sharp ridge
through deep snow. On the precipice side, the snow
had been piled by the wind in overhanging slabs
called cornices. These might be roughly likened to

the tiles of a roof which overlap the edge of a house. To tread upon them would be to plunge thousands of feet to instant death. Hillary and Tensing would have to keep as close to the edge of the ridge as possible to reach the peak, and yet be careful not to walk unwittingly on the cornices of snow which would give way under their weight.

In its final defense against men, the Goddess Mother of the World had set up a grim hurdle. Much would depend upon weather and the condition of Hillary and Tensing when they reached the south summit and started climbing the final ridge to the peak. Death or victory both lay waiting for them and none could say, until the issue was put to the test, on which side the scales would be weighted.

Bourdillon and Evans made their way slowly down to the camp on the South Col. The strenuous climb of some three thousand feet in under five hours had taken a heavy toll upon them. They could move only haltingly on uncertain limbs and were staggering when they reached the gully which led to the South Col.

In the meantime, Colonel Hunt with his one Sherpa porter, Da Namgyal, had been toiling up Everest behind Evans and Bourdillon, intent upon setting up Camp Eight, from which Hillary and Tensing were to make their attempt.

Hunt was able to climb only at a snail's pace and found himself gasping for breath despite his oxygen apparatus. Although he did not know it until later, a block of ice had formed in the exhaust tube of his oxygen set, so he was getting little oxygen to help him. After every few steps he had to stop and fight for air in order to go on. At last, the two got to the camp in which Lambert and Tensing had spent their frightful night, slapping each other to keep their blood circulating, during the Swiss attempt of the previous year.

It was apparent to Colonel Hunt that in his condition, and with only one porter, he would not be
able actually to set up Camp Eight. The best that
could be done would be to carry the stores as high
as possible and then dump them. The camp itself
have to be erected by the support party which would
provide backing for Hillary and Tensing.

The two struggled on for another two hundred feet.
They now estimated that they were at twenty-seven
thousand three hundred and fifty feet, and could go
no further. Ahead the ridge steepened, providing no
camp site, and so they dumped their stores where
they were. Then they built up a mound of snow to
mark the spot and staggered down to the South Col.
To provide an extra supply for Hillary and Tensing,
they took off their oxygen bottles and left them with
the stores. That meant making the descent without
oxygen, and the lack of it soon made itself felt.

It had commenced to snow, and a wind, thin and
piercing cold, whipped up from the west. Senses were
numbed. Breathing became more labored than ever.
Their progress down the mountain was dangerously
slow, punctuated by slips and falls. By now Hillary
and Tensing had arrived at Camp Seven on the South
Col. They saw Hunt and Da Namgyal creeping down
in an exhausted condition and went up to meet them
and help them in. Then they revived them with hot
drinks and learned where the stores had been dumped
for them. Two hours later, Evans and Bourdillon
reached Camp Seven also.

In a few hours it would be the turn of Hillary and
Tensing to pit their courage, their strength, their skill,
and their will power against the still unconquered peak
of Everest.

EVEREST NOW SUMMONED TO HER DEFENSE
the fiercest of her weapons. The wind, which had
started blowing strongly as Bourdillon and Evans
fought their way down off the mountain after their
record-breaking climb, now piped up out of the west
in a full gale. It blew all night, so that none in Camp
Seven on the South Col could get any rest. The following day, when Tensing and Hillary were to make their
bid for the summit, a gale still flung across the South
Col, howling past the peaks around, now roaring and
now whistling, and bringing with it a hail of flying
snow and slivers of ice.

There was nothing for it but to delay the effort to
the following day, May 28. The delay, meaning that
the climbers and their support party must spend another twenty-four hours on the inhospitable tableland
of ice which constitutes the South Col, was sure to tell
upon them.

The wind blew at gale force all through the day, so
that even so small a journey as passing from one tent
to another chilled a man to the bone. Food was difficult to prepare. Limbs, lacking exercise, grew cold and
cramped, and altitude began to take some effect.

Lowe and Gregory, with three Sherpas, Angnima,
Angtemba, and Pembar, were to make the support
party for Hillary and Tensing. Their job would be to

carry stores and extra oxygen for them up to Camp
Eight. They would then return to the South Col
camp, leaving Hillary and Tensing to set up the camp
and spend the night there. But Angtemba and Pembar succumbed to altitude sickness. That left only
three men to carry loads intended to be taken by five.
There was only one thing for it. The climbers themselves would have to carry loads. That would put an
extra drain upon their energy and the strength which
they would need to achieve the peak. But it was either
that or call the venture off, and that was not to be
thought of.

The morning of May 28 was relatively calm. The
loads for Camp Eight were repacked, and all that
could possibly be done without discarded. Then Lowe,
Gregory and Angnima set off ahead of Hillary and
Tensing for Camp Eight. Hillary and Tensing followed later and in excellent climbing weather all managed to reach the place where Colonel Hunt and Da
Namgyal had dumped their load for Camp Eight two
days previously.

It was decided that this spot was too low, and the
camp would have to be established higher up if there
was to be any hope of Hillary and Tensing reaching
the summit. But this meant that each would have to
carry more gear. Angnima, plucky but not in as good
condition as the others, was given a forty pound load
to pack. Hillary, Tensing, Lowe, and Gregory each
took loads weighing fifty to sixty pounds on their
backs. The grade ahead was much steeper and progress more slow. Steps had to be cut in places—a
tiring job at the best of times, but exhausting work at
over twenty-seven thousand feet and with a heavy
load to carry. At last all reached a spot which was
estimated at twenty-seven thousand nine hundred
feet. It was not level. The best that could be said of

it was that it was less steep than anywhere else around. Hillary decided that Camp Eight would be set up here. Lowe, Gregory, and Angnima dumped their loads, wished the climbers luck, and left for the South Col. Hillary and Tensing set about erecting their tent.

First, some kind of platform had to be made for it. To save their oxygen—for due to the sickness of the porters, they had not as many cylinders as they hoped for—the two took off their breathing apparatus to get by as best they could on the thin air of the mountain. Scraping and shoveling away the snow, they at last burrowed down to a rocky surface which lay at a not-too-steep angle. In the frozen rock, working with their ice axes and pausing frequently for breath, they leveled a tiny space on which the tent could be pitched. Actually it was not possible to level one complete area. They had to make, as it were, two small steps, and pitch the tent over these. Each step was about three feet wide and six feet long, one a foot above the other. Over these the tent was pitched and secured as strongly as possible. Then Hillary and Tensing made dinner of hot tea and cocoa, crackers, canned apricots, dates, sardines, honey, and jam—a strange menu but tastes at something over five miles up are strange, and men who normally would be revolted by honey and sardines find them quite to their liking.

Because they were short of oxygen, the men could use only enough for four hours each during the night. They had intended to breathe oxygen all night while sleeping because tests had shown that a good rest could be obtained this way. However, with but four hours supply available for each, they used the oxygen in two two-hour periods, from 9 to 11 P.M. and from 1 to 3 A.M. When the oxygen was on, they were able to doze. But when the supply was cut off, both became wakeful, cold, and tired. Tensing slept in the lower berth, quite undisturbed by the fact that if he rolled over off his air mattress, he would not stop until he was two or three miles further down the mountain. Hillary half lay, half sat in the upper berth, holding on to the sides of the tent when a gust of wind sprang up to keep it on the ground. In this way both passed a cheerless night. The following morning they prepared a breakfast of more sardines and crackers, drank quantities of lemon juice and sugar, and after checking their oxygen, set off at 6:30.

It was the best of days. The sky was clear, there was little or no wind, and every hope that this time the summit would be reached.

Tensing led the way for the first hundred feet of climbing, kicking steps in the soft snow for Hillary to follow. They planned to keep as close to the ridge as they could but when they got to it, Hillary found it as sharp almost as a knife-edge and thickly beset with cornices of snow. So, taking the lead, Hillary chose a path just below the ridge. Here the wind had formed a crust upon the snow which at times supported them and at others broke under their weight.

Quite abruptly, the knife edge of the ridge dissolved into a tiny hollow, and at the bottom of this, the two found two oxygen bottles. These were the ones left by Bourdillon and Evans who had taken them off so that Hillary and Tensing might have a better chance of reaching the summit. Grateful for the extra supply, they left the cylinders where they were to be picked up on the way back.

They were now four hundred feet from the top of the south summit. The ridge along which they had been climbing was replaced by a formidable mound of soft snow. Cautiously the two men climbed up this, roped together and alert for any sign of avalanche. But the snow held and by nine o'clock, three and a half hours out from Camp Eight, they were on top of the south summit.

Here they changed their oxygen bottles, throwing away their used ones, which were now empty. This reduced their load to nineteen pounds each. But they were on their last bottle, apart from the half empty ones which Bourdillon and Evans had left for them. They would have to move fast and use less oxygen than had been originally planned.

Before them now lay the final frightful ridge to the summit. It rose steeply and presented a choice of two dangerous routes. Along the knife edge of the ridge was deep snow which overhung the precipice on the other side. This might slide, or, if they went out too far upon it, give way, hurling them down some twelve thousand feet to a glacier below. Where the snow ended there was a jagged mass of rocks which would make the most difficult kind of climbing. These rocks had but one thing in their favor. On the north side of Everest, as mentioned in previous chapters, the rocks sloped outward and downward so that to try to get a foothold on them was like trying to creep along the tiles of a steep roof. On this side the rocks jutted upwards, presenting a better surface for climbing.

Hillary, examining the obstacles ahead from the south summit, believed that it was just possible that where the snow joined the rocks, it might have been frozen by the wind into a crust which would be hard enough to cut steps in. They badly needed some kind of steps or purchase for their feet. The ridge up which they must climb to the tip of Everest was desperately steep. And it fell away so sharply that balancing was no easy task.

With oxygen running short, they had no time for

speculation. Hillary led the attack on the ridge, and his hopes soared when his ice axe bit into the snow, clean and firm, so that with a stroke or two he was able to cut a step big enough for his huge climbing boots to fit in. If luck held, the snow would be firm like this to the summit and that would make much easier this final crucial part of the climb, in which victory or disaster lay in the balance.

Hillary was roped to Tensing by a forty foot line and because the slope they were to climb was so steep, and also because the snow of Everest had proved so treacherous in the past, the two worked out a plan which would give them a chance of survival should either slip. First Hillary cut steps for the full length of the line, that is to say, for forty feet. Tensing in the meantime drove his ice axe into the snow and took a few turns of the rope around it. Thus if Hillary slipped, Tensing would have a chance of holding him.

Then Tensing would climb up to Hillary and take his turn cutting steps for another forty feet, with Hillary anchoring him in case of accident. In this way they made good progress. But now and then they had to detour to avoid big cornices, and at times the slope was so steep that hand holds as well as steps had to be cut in the snow.

At one point, when Tensing had come up to Hillary, the latter noted that he seemed extremely tired and was breathing with the greatest difficulty though he made no complaint. Hillary himself was feeling quite fresh and suspected that something had gone wrong with Tensing's oxygen set. He examined it and found that there was a block of ice about two inches in diameter in the exhaust tube of his breathing apparatus. That meant that he was getting hardly any oxygen at all. It was the same kind of blockage which had occurred in Colonel Hunt's set a few days previously. Hilary cleared the ice away, and thereafter kept a watch to see that the tubes were free of ice. So small a circumstance as that could spell defeat.

Once, the better to examine the way ahead, Hillary took off his snow goggles for a second. Immediately he was all but blinded by fine particles of ice, quite invisible, which were being driven by the wind across the lonely crest of the mountain. He replaced his goggles in a hurry and did not take them off again.

After an hour of climbing, Hillary and Tensing came to a rock, forty feet high, blocking their route to the summit. It was not an unexpected obstacle, for they had seen it many times before from below through binoculars. But they had hoped that there would be some way around or over it. Now, at close quarters, they realized that it was quite impossible to climb the rock in less than several hours. It was completely without holds of any kind—a sheer slab of stone, rising forty feet above them like a wall. There was only one possibility of surmounting it—a possibility which, if anything went wrong, could mean death for both of them.

Between the rock and the precipice on the right hand side was a huge snow cornice—a mound or pillar of snow which overhung the edge of the mountain. A crack, just large enough to allow a man to insert himself into it, lay between this snow cornice and the rock. One climber might be able to squirm and struggle up this crack to the top. But there was the risk that in so doing, the cornice would topple off the precipice, carrying the climber with it.

Hillary told Tensing to make the end of his rope fast around his ice axe in a firm belay. Then he squeezed himself into the crack. He had crampons on his boots. Doubling his legs behind him, he managed to dig these into the snow and start pushing himself slowly upward. Foot after foot he ascended in the crack, cramped, gasping for breath, expecting that at any moment the snow would topple off the mountain taking him with it. But the snow held and at last Hillary reached the top of the rock, triumphant, but so out of breath that he had to lie down for a few minutes. Then he pulled in the rope as Tensing wriggled up the crack after him.

The two looked at each other and grinned. Tensing seemed to be moving a little slowly and Hillary asked him how he was. For reply, the dauntless Sherpa waved on towards the peak. Nothing would stop them now.

They set out again. Once more they faced the danger of a series of cornices which had to be carefully negotiated, one cutting steps and the other anchoring him. As they surmounted each mound of snow and rock, they hoped it would be the last. But another always lay ahead. The ridge curved around to the right, with a series of humps to be negotiated. One of these surely would be the summit. And yet the summit never seemed to be reached. They were moving slowly now. Oxygen was running low. They had not much more time and Hillary wondered how much he could cut down the oxygen and still be safe.

Then Hillary realized with a jolt of excitement that the ridge ahead instead of rising above them sloped DOWN! He was stooped over cutting steps and raised his head. Below lay the East Rongbuk Glacier. He could see over to the other side of Everest. Trembling with excitement, he straightened up and looked around. A narrow ridge of snow rose upwards a few feet ahead of him to a sharp summit.

THIS WAS THE PEAK OF EVEREST!

A few paces more and they were both on it, triumphant, standing together on the highest spot in the

world which so many before them had failed to reach.
The time was 11:30 A.M. They had been climbing for
five hours.

For a moment they experienced little but a sense of
relief that the long ordeal of climbing and of cutting
steps in the snow was over. Then Hillary held out his
hand, and these two men from such different backgrounds, of such widely separate races and religious
beliefs, shook hands, grinning from ear to ear, on the
top of the world.

The handshake was the natural reaction of the Brit-
isher, Hillary. But for Tensing it was not enough. He
flung his arms around Hillary and the two pounded
each other on the back until they had to let up for
want of breath.

Hillary then took off his oxygen set and photo-
graphed Tensing standing on the peak of the Goddess
Mother of the World, holding on his ice axe handle
the flags of Britain, Nepal (where Tensing was born),
India where he lived, and the United Nations. He took
pictures of the splendid and awesome view from the
highest point on the surface of the world. But his
hands became clumsy and his coordination bad due to
lack of oxygen.

Tensing, in the meantime, performed a small and
touching devotion of his own. Of the Buddhist faith,
he believed that Mount Everest is the home of some
of the gods of his religion. So he made a hole in the
snow and placed a few simple offerings there for his
gods—a bar of chocolate, a handful of biscuits, and
some candy.

The two remained about fifteen minutes on the
summit. They searched for signs of Mallory and
Irvine, but found none. Then they took one last look
round at the North Col, from which so many attempts
had been made, at the great gully where Norton and

others had been turned back, and the steep northeast ridge where Mallory and Irvine were last seen. All the giant mountains around seemed but hills far below their feet. Then it was time to turn back.

Both were very tired, far more tired than they knew, and as they descended the wind, mercifully withheld until now, sprang up. They had to hurry because oxygen was running short. At their tiny tent they picked up their sleeping bags and mattresses and headed for Camp Seven on the South Col. They scrambled over rocks, moved singly over sections covered with snow, and took every care lest death or accident snatch the victory from them.

The wind had obliterated their carefully stamped steps on the great snow gully down to the South Col, and exhausted as they were, they had to cut more. Hillary cut first and then Tensing. At one place they found they could walk down, slowly trusting to their crampons for safety. Gusts of wind threatened to bowl them over. But at last, barely able to put one foot before the other, they were met by Noyce and Lowe who brought them hot soup and emergency oxygen. This revived them sufficiently to get to the South Col camp. And there, over a meal of omelet and mugs of hot lemonade, the two told the story of their great triumph.

CHAPTER TWENTY-FOUR
The Real Victors

THE NEWS THAT MOUNT EVEREST HAD AT last been climbed was flashed around the world within a few hours of Tensing and Hillary returning from the summit. It reached Queen Elizabeth II of Great Britain upon the eve of her glittering coronation—a tribute, as it were, to the queen whom many Britons hope will follow in the footsteps of her great predecessor, Queen Elizabeth I.

She conferred knighthood on both Colonel Hunt, leader of the expedition, and upon Hillary. To Tensing went the award of the George Medal—Britain's highest award for a civilian. Since Tensing was not a British subject, the question of honoring him further would have to be taken up with the government of Nepal to ensure that no offense would be unwittingly given.

The two returned from the mountain to be greeted by demonstrations such as have rarely been afforded any men in modern times. They were met by ceremonial devil dancers and by members of the British Embassy in Nepal. They were smothered with flowers and covered with kumkum, a red powder of rejoicing given by the Nepalese to their greatest heroes. The state coach of King Tribhuvan, ruler of Nepal, carried them through the streets of Katmandu, the capital of that country, for an audience with the King himself. And from all quarters of the globe, the cables and messages of congratulations showered upon them.

As far back as the early 1920's the Mount Everest Committee in London had given serious thought to a proposal that the names of those who eventually achieved the top of Everest be withheld. The Committee had in mind that all who took part in any expedition against Everest would contribute towards its eventual conquest. Therefore, no one or two men should be singled out for special glory.

Such a plan, even if advisable, was certainly not workable. The world, it was realized, would never allow the names of those who reached the top of the highest mountain to be kept secret.

But this book has failed in a major purpose if it has not made clear that the summit of the highest mountain in the world was achieved, from the very start, by team work. All who ventured against the mountain are sharers in the glory of its winning, from the early pundit explorers, risking their lives in a forbidden country, to Dr. Kellas, who died within sight of the Goddess Mother of the World, Captain Noel, Norton, Mallory, and Irvine, who lost their lives somewhere on its gale-stricken wastes, the seven porters killed in the avalanche of 1924, Somervell, Odell, Bullock, Tilman, Harris, Shipton, Lambert and his Swiss companions— through all the list of Everest adventurers, Tibetan and Nepalese porters as well as Europeans.

Hillary and Tensing themselves were the first to acknowledge this fact, knowing that they had, as essential allies in their victorious climb, the experience, the courage, and the hardships endured by a host of others.

Everest was not won by two men, but by the spirit of mankind—a spirit which, though rebuffed many times, has proved indomitable in the face of all the tasks with which it has been confronted.

It is not that man has climbed the highest mountain in the world that makes the Everest story an epic. Rather, it is that man would not give up his efforts to do so, even in the face of death, until he was victorious.

Summit - 29,002'

Hillary & Tensing, 1953

Bourdillon & Evans,
1953 - 28,700'

Mallory & Irvine, 1924
last seen here
28,000'

Lambert & Tensing,
1952 - 28,215'

North Col -
22,990'

South Col -
25,850'

Highest point (28,100')
reached by Norton - 1924:
Wager, Harris, Smythe - 1933.

Principal Personnel of
Everest Expeditions

THE RECONNAISSANCE OF 1921

Lieutenant Colonel C. K. Howard-Bury, *leader*
Dr. A. M. Kellas, *assistant leader*
A. F. R. Wollaston, *assistant leader*
Harold Raeburn, *leader of climbers*
G. H. Bullock, *climber*
George H. Leigh-Mallory, *climber*
Major H. T. Morshead, *surveyor*
Major E. O. Wheeler, *surveyor*
Dr. A. Heron, *geologist*

ATTEMPT OF 1922

Brigadier General C. G. Bruce, *leader*
Lieutenant Colonel E. L. Strutt, *assistant leader*
George H. Leigh-Mallory, *climber*
Captain George Finch, *climber and oxygen expert*
Major E. F. Norton, *climber*
Dr. Howard Somervell, *medical officer*
Dr. Wakefield, *medical officer*
Captain Geoffrey Bruce, *climber and transport officer*
Dr. T. G. Longstaff, *medical officer and naturalist*
Captain J. B. L. Noel, *photographer*
C. G. Crawford, *climber*
Major H. T. Morshead, *geologist and climber*
Captain C. G. Morris, *transport officer*

ATTEMPT OF 1924

Brigadier General C. G. Bruce, *leader*
Major E. F. Norton, *assistant leader*

George H. Leigh-Mallory, *climber*
Captain Geoffrey Bruce, *climber*
E. O. Shebbeare, *transport officer*
Major R. W. G. Hingston, *medical officer*
Dr. T. H. Somervell, *medical officer*
N .E. Odell, *oxygen expert and geologist*
Bentley Beetham, *climber*
J. De Vere Hazard, *climber*
Andrew Irvine, *climber*
Captain J. B. L. Noel, *photographer*

ATTEMPT OF 1933

Hugh Ruttledge, *leader*
C. G. Crawford, *climber*
F. S. Smythe, *climber*
Eric E. Shipton, *climber*
Dr. Raymond Greene, *medical officer*
Captain E. St. J. Birnie, *climber*
Wyn Harris, *climber*
L. R. Wager, *climber*
J. L. Longland, *climber*
Major Hugh Boustead, *climber*
Dr. W. McLean, *medical officer*
George Wood Johnson, *climber*
T. A. Brocklebank, *climber*
E .O. Shebbeare, *transport officer*

RECONNAISSANCE OF 1935

Eric E. Shipton, *leader*
H. W. Tilman, *climber*
Dr. C. B. M. Warren, *medical officer*
Edwin G. H. Kempson, *climber*
E. H. L. Wigram, *climber*
L. V. Bryant, *climber*
Michael Spender, *surveyor*

ATTEMPT OF 1936

Hugh Ruttledge, *leader*
F. S. Smythe, *climber*
Eric E. Shipton, climber
Wyn Harris, *climber*

Edwin G. H. Kempson, *climber*
Dr. C. B. M. Warren, *medical officer*
E. H. L. Wigram, *climber*
P. R. Oliver, *climber*
J. M. L. Gavin, *climber*
C. J. Morris, *transportation officer*
W. R. Smyth-Windham, *radio officer*
G. Noel Humphreys, *medical officer*

ATTEMPT OF 1938

Harold W. Tilman, *leader*
F. S. Smythe, *climber*
N. E. Odell, *climber*
Eric E. Shipton, *climber*
Dr. C. B. M. Warren, *medical officer*
Peter Lloyd, *climber*
P. R. Oliver, *climber*

RECONNAISSANCE OF 1951

Eric E. Shipton, *leader*
W. H. Murray, *climber*
Michael Ward, *climber*
Thomas Bourdillon, *climber*
Edmund P. Hillary, *climber*
H. E. Riddiford, *climber*
Dr. Dutt, *geologist*

SWISS ATTEMPT, SPRING OF 1952

Dr. Wyss-Dunant, *leader*
André Roch, *climber*
Raymond Lambert, *climber*
René Dittert, *climber*
Dr. Gabriel Chevalley, *climber*
René Aubert, *climber*
Léon Flory, *climber*
Jean-Jacques Asper, *climber*
Ernest Hofstetter, *climber*
Professor A. Lombard, *geologist*
A. Zimmermann, *botanist*
Madame Lobsiger-Dellenbach, *ethnographer*
Tensing Bhutia, *climber*

SWISS ATTEMPT, FALL OF 1952

Dr. Gabriel Chevalley, *leader*
Raymond Lambert, *climber*
Tensing Bhutia, *climber*
Jean Buzio, *climber*
Ernst Reiss, *climber*
Gustav Gross, *climber*
Arthur Spöhel, *climber*
Professor Norman Dyhrenfurth, *photographer (American)*

BRITISH ATTEMPT, SPRING OF 1952

Col. Henry C. J. Hunt, *leader*
C. G. Band, *climber*
T. D. Bourdillon, *climber*
Edmund P. Hillary, *climber*
Tensing Bhutia, *climber*
R. C. Evans, *climber*
W. G. Lowe, *climber*
C. W. F. Noyce, *climber*
A. Gregory, *climber*
Dr. L. G. C. Pugh, *physiologist*
T. Stobart, *photographer*
Dr. M. P. Ward, *medical officer*
M. H. Westmacott, *climber*
Major C. G. Wylie, *organizing secretary*

Bibliography

Arranged Chronologically

Mount Everest, the Reconnaissance, 1921 by Lt. Col. C. K. Howard-Bury, DSO and other members of the expedition. (New York: Longmans, Green & Company, 1922.)

The Assault on Mount Everest, 1922 by the Hon. C. G. Bruce and other members of the expedition. (New York: Longmans, Green & Company, 1923.)

The Story of Everest by John Baptist Lucius Noel (Boston: Little Brown & Company, 1927.)

The Fight for Everest: 1924 by Lt. Col. E. F. Norton, DSO (New York: Longmans, Green & Company, 1925.)

The Epic of Mount Everest by Sir Francis Younghusband (New York: Longmans, Green & Company, 1926.)

Everest: the Challenge by Sir Francis Younghusband (New York: Thomas Nelson & Sons, 1936.)

Attack on Everest by Hugh Ruttledge (New York: Robert M. McBride & Company, 1935.)

Everest, the Unfinished Adventure (1936) by Hugh Ruttledge (London: Hodder and Stoughton, 1937.)

Mount Everest, 1938 by Harold W. Tilman (Cambridge: Cambridge University Press, 1948.)

The Mount Everest Reconnaissance Expedition, 1951

by Eric Shipton (London: Hodder and Stoughton, 1952.)

The Story of Everest by William H. Murray (New York: E. P. Dutton & Company, 1953.)

The Mountain Vision by F. S. Smythe (London: Hodder and Stoughton, 1941.)

Life Magazine, issue of June 29, 1953.

The Times, (London) Mount Everest Supplement, July, 1953.

more good reading in

THE LAUREL-LEAF LIBRARY